MW00935246

"Tom Tunnicliff has m
with both young peopl
he is well equipped to address a significant issue
namely how do we encourage young people to
develop into mature leaders."
Stuart Briscoe, Pastor Emeritus, Elmbrook
Church, noted author, conference speaker,
pastor to pastors.

"This book highlights critical factors for the
development of leaders who can face the
challenges of a complex culture. The personal
anecdotes, stories from the lives of other leaders
and contemporary research kept me engaged. I
think the best reference I can give is that I will
be passing on a copy to my children with my
strong encouragement to read and apply the
lessons in their own parenting."
Scott Arbeiter, President, World Relief

"Tom Tunnicliff will ignite the future of many
who read his book about how leaders become
leaders. He creates a life map for all of us by
describing the journeys of a number of
successful pastors and people in ministry. But
he doesn't stop there, he gives us practical steps
to follow to determine how we have arrived to
our place in Christian ministry, and possible
next steps. Thank you, Tom, I will use your
book in my ministry!"
Mark E. Johnson, President of Life Channel
Coaching, Church planter and Life Coach for
pastors and church planters

"Through interviews of over forty high-impact ministry leaders, Dr. Tom Tunnicliff uncovers four distinct layers of confidence that emerge over varied stages and experiences of a person's life. Tom illustrates that when these layers of confidence are combined with the "glue" of four key character qualities, the fruit is greater impact and effectiveness in life and leadership. Filled with stories, research and personal anecdotes, Tom's book takes you on a journey that will challenge you to reflect on your own life-journey as a person and leader as well as on your impact you can have on the lives of people under your influence. I recommend Tom's book especially to those in ministry who are leading and serving future generations of leaders."

Tom Keppeler,
Executive Director, Prism Economic Development Corporation

"I loved the stories of pastors and their life lessons as they grew in their capacity to lead. The whole layout of the concept of confidence was easy to grasp and apply as we develop leaders among us here at Lakeside."

Brad Franklin, Senior Pastor Lakeside Church

IGNITING FUTURE

Igniting Future

How To Build People
Of High Impact

By Tom Tunnicliff

Igniting Future
How To Build People Of High Impact
Published by Kindle Direct Publications

U.S.A.

ISBN (trade paper): 978-1-73115-590-0

Version 2.0

Edited by Neil Wilson

Cover design: Sheila Hahn

Special Thanks

I want to give special thanks to the many people who helped me along the way to get this book into print.

Thank you to all forty of the senior pastors in my initial research who took the time and energy to share their stories about what happened to help to build them into people of high impact.

Thank you to Ray Johnston at Bayside Church for your encouragement and help to launch my first stage of research among megachurch senior pastors.

Thank you to my USC professor and advisor, Bill Tierney, whose guidance and counsel increased the quality of my foundational research and writing tenfold.

Thank you to Warren and Mary Widicus who gave me an incredible location to write this book.

Thank you to Mel Lawrenz for his friendship and technical expertise to get this and my previous book into print.

And the final thank you to my incredible wife Kirsten and my three kids, Hunter, Hannah, Hudson, and daughter-in-law, Brenna, for all the love and life lessons learned in the crucible of Family.

Contents

ESSENTIAL CONCLUDING THOUGHTS

INTRODUCTION

Few things get a kid's juices flowing like an upcoming trip to the Magic Kingdom. As a boy growing up two hours north of L.A., I would start hyperventilating just thinking about our family's next trip to Disneyland. Sunday nights watching the *Wonderful World of Disney* – long before there was cable – fueled my imagination months before our vacation.

Referencing the map of the Magic Kingdom pinned to my bedroom wall, I frequently described my most recent adventures in *Tomorrowland* to other neighborhood kids. For me, *Tomorrowland* was almost intoxicating. It was a place where I could catch a glimpse of a future where anything was possible; take a rocket to the moon or shrink to the size of a molecule; a future where a ten-year-old's human potential knew no limits! Today I wonder how to recapture that boundless outlook. If only that kind of *Disney-Like* anticipation would show up the week before my son's class project is due, or infect my new students on the first day of class.

Years ago I regularly taught an introduction to graduate school course. Inevitably, just three weeks into the semester it became obvious which students were most likely to flourish and which would have a more difficult go of it. Something was noticeably different about the high performing students. They seemed almost pre-wired to thrive. They were good students, had great people skills, were articulate, and just easy to be around. Many were already working full-time or as interns in meaningful jobs.

The students who were seemingly primed to succeed provoked my thinking. Why do some kids grow up to be world-changers and really make a difference while others just coast? What takes place in their childhoods that doesn't happen in others' upbringing? Why is it that some young people have seemingly unstoppable upward momentum while others plateau or derail early? Is it family background, better schools, extra-curricular choices, the right timing, or are they just born with high-impact DNA?

These questions about the impact of nature or nurture aren't new, but the answers remain elusive. According to one study, "Much leadership talent is hard-wired in people before they reach their early to mid-twenties.... Simply put, people do not change very much once they enter the corporate world, and the changes that do occur are mainly a consolidation of strengths..."[1]

The more I pondered these questions, the more fascinated I became by the mystery of it. If there was a pattern to how leadership talent gets hard-wired in someone before their early twenties, I wanted to discover it.

My quest to understand this hard-wiring phenomenon led me to undertake a nationwide study to interview organizational leaders who have high-impact track records.[2] I simply wanted to ask them what happened in their lives, particularly in their early years prior to college graduation that influenced their personal growth. So for the first set of interviews I chose forty megachurch pastors,[3] each of whom demonstrated a long-term record of leadership success[4] and led congregations with two thousand to twenty-two thousand attendees.[5] I figured that if you can build a volunteer organization to over two thousand members you have got to have something going for you.

I had a hunch that the abilities and strengths that have carried these remarkable individuals to the top of their professions – are nurtured earlier rather than later in life. Common patterns emerged in these interviews as all forty described what experiences influenced them most during their formative years in high school, college, and post-college early career.

One pattern, one transformational experience rose above all others – (building) the development of confidence, --layers upon layers of confidence. Not just an *"I-can-tie-my-shoes-all-by-myself"* assurance, but one that revealed itself in recognizable layers. These **layers of confidence** were accumulated and established in the early years, even though the seeds for growing that confidence were planted younger.

As these layers start to form, they stack up and create an expanding ability to influence others, as shown in this diagram:

4 LAYERS OF CONFIDENCE

There are four distinct layers of confidence. The first layer, Primitive Confidence, is foundational and forms before the other three. With its first DNA-like reinforcing factors (RF) developing during elementary and middle school, primitive confidence grows strongest during the high school and college years. The three other layers are forged repeatedly throughout those early years and beyond.

Together, these layers of confidence make a person stronger and bring about a lasting change and growth. The more layers of confidence, the greater the capacity to impact others. One of the most vivid examples of how these four layers work to bring about this change can be seen in what builders commonly know as wooden glulam beams...

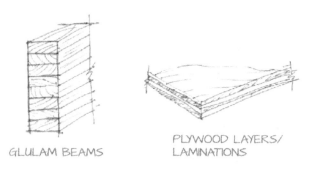

GLULAM BEAMS   PLYWOOD LAYERS/
                        LAMINATIONS

I was introduced to glulams as a young and enthusiastic architectural student. During a lecture on wood beams, a light bulb came on as the professor described the physics of glulam beams. A glulam is a large wood beam made up of laminated wood pieces, bonded together with super strong glue. Pound for pound, a glulam beam is stronger than steel.[6] A glulam looks like a stack of two-by-fours glued together to make one massive beam. The more laminations or *layers*, the greater the load it can carry, the greater force it can withstand, and the more prominent role it can play in a building's structural design. A sheet of plywood also follows this pattern. The more layers or laminations of wood, the stronger the plywood. Similarly, the more layers of confidence a person possesses, the greater their capacity to withstand and overcome outside forces, influence others, and make a difference. Note, in the figures below, how the weight (represented by arrows) reveals the beam's capacity to carry a load.

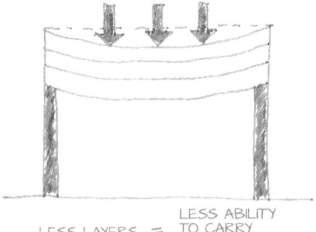

LESS LAYERS = LESS ABILITY TO CARRY HEAVY LOADS

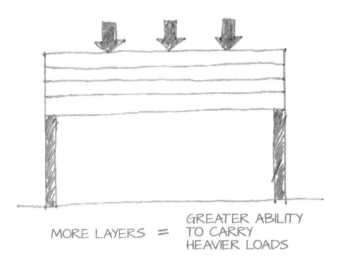

MORE LAYERS = GREATER ABILITY TO CARRY HEAVIER LOADS

For Stuart Briscoe, the noted author, conference speaker, and innovative pastor, withstanding and overcoming outside forces in high school came as a by-product of his athletic success. Born and raised in England, Stuart was forced to deal with the stigma of being a religious outsider in his own country. According to Briscoe, "You were either a Catholic, Church of England, or you were something strange."[7] In the Brethren Church he grew up in, "we were really marked people in the small town where we lived."[8] It was his love for rugby and cricket that helped him overcome the religious stigma. He excelled in both, gaining recognition and respect from fellow students for his intensity and skill on the field. As a result, he gained layers of confidence – a humble confidence – that followed him into his widely influential career.

Often, acquiring new layers of confidence leads to an expanded sphere of influence. This phenomenon is illustrated by the inverted pyramid in the following figure.

Over the span of a person's career, as confidence is built in one season of life, it is common to experience an expansion to more responsibility and a greater sphere of influence in the following season. On the flip side, as new layers of confidence develop over time, the skill set one uses to make a difference becomes narrower, focused, and sharpened around specific leadership capacities.[9] The skills and knowledge needed at the start of a career are not the same ones needed mid to late career.[10]

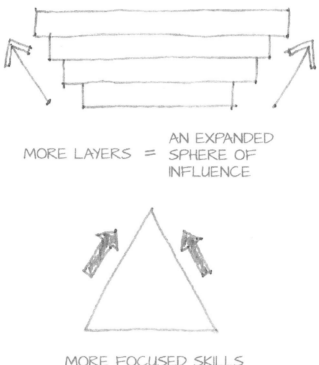

MORE LAYERS = AN EXPANDED SPHERE OF INFLUENCE

MORE FOCUSED SKILLS OVER TIME

Just out of college, one of my first big projects as a new architect was a major custom home remodel. To handle this job, I had to possess certain technical skills like construction fundamentals, sketching, drawing, and drafting. As we got under way, I also found myself functioning as the referee in more than one owner-versus-contractor conflict. One of those conflicts involved what I called *The Stairway from Hell.*

I designed this relatively simple staircase and sketched it in 2D and 3D, including the smallest details. The owner looked at the drawings and said "Looks great. Go for it!"

Halfway through construction I received a frantic call from the contractor telling me that the owner had stopped all work on the job because the stairs were wrong. I ran down to the jobsite and after a painfully detailed review, found that the stairs were built exactly according to plans -- the same plans the owner had approved.

The problem was that once he saw the staircase actually built, he didn't like it. So we started over. It wasn't until our third attempt that we completed the stairs to the owner's satisfaction. At this point, the contractor's blood pressure skyrocketed anytime the owner's truck pulled into the driveway.

Years later, when I think of all the time and energy I invested to finish that project, I realize that I used ninety percent of my technical skills on designing and redoing the work and just ten percent of my people skills on resolving the conflict.

In later years, with more experience and confidence, those percentages were reversed. By mid-career, I was using ninety percent of my people skills for client relations and just ten percent of my technical skills, usually while overseeing others' projects. Experiences like the *Stairway from Hell* helped me build layers of confidence while working with others. Over time, my sphere of influence expanded and my abilities became more focused on people skills (see the following figure).

So why is it that some kids grow up and become world-changers? Is it because they developed solid layers of confidence?

Yes, *but that's not the whole story.* There is something else, another element that comes into play, something that cements long-term growth. That something is the addition of epoxy-like seams (ELS).

These epoxy-like seams (ELS) are character qualities that act like the glue holding together the wood layers of a glulam beam or a sheet of plywood. Without incredibly strong glue, glulam beams don't function to their full capacity and will fail. Without effective ELS's, individuals may grow up without achieving their full potential or might lack important abilities that will help them flourish.

There are four specific ELS's that influence the forming of the four layers of confidence and their inter-cohesiveness. They are so pivotal to this whole process that an entire chapter is devoted to each one.

4 EPOXY- LIKE SEAMS

People who make a difference in the world are not simply the products of cosmic forces outside their reach. Early in life rather than later, high impact people develop these almost embryonic ELS's while layers of confidence are forming. The constantly morphing results create an even greater capability to live an outwardly focused life of impact and influence.

What we hope to do in every chapter of this book is to help you and those you influence learn how to intentionally develop these layers of confidence and accompanying ELS's to full capacity.

As a big college football fan, I love the beginning of the season where most teams start at full capacity. But games decimate the ranks. A handful of injuries can soon have the team operating well below full capacity. However, the next season rolls around and with solid off-season training and good recruiting your team is back to full capacity.

This book is about helping you reach your full capacity, by preparing you to help those you influence reach their full potential. For many who step into new roles of influence like a coach, a teacher, or a youth pastor, insecurities and lack of confidence can threaten to undermine moving towards full capacity: "I'm not like the last coach;" "I'm not as good as the last teacher;" or "The youth pastor before me was like a rock star." For some, a lack of know-how and basic skills can undermine confidence as well: "I'm not sure I have what it takes."

On the personal side of this study in leadership, *full capacity* isn't the first phrase I would use to describe my own parental trajectory. My wife Kirsten and I consider ourselves the *better-late-than-never* family. We were married at thirty, had our first child at thirty-five, our last at forty and added our dog (who we loved, but had serious emotional issues) at forty-four. Every season has provided pitfalls to humble us, joys to inspire us, and opportunities to propel us.
During each of the pre-kids, little kids, and big kids phases of our life, we have always found time to visit Disneyland. As nostalgic as the park is to me, it is always changing, and the experience does not remain the same.

The *Tomorrowland* I grew up with was a place where I could see the future and dream about things to come. During our last trip, we found that *Tomorrowland* had been remodeled once again, with older, familiar attractions removed to make room for newer versions of the future. Today, it still is a place to inspire dreams – not the same dreams of my childhood, but new dreams for new kids.

While I may not be able to return to the *Tomorrowland* of my youth, I'm OK with that, because it has led me to a new dream that I can change the future. I can *ignite future* through the next generation who can *change the world*, one person at a time.

I don't believe I've met anyone who does not want to make a real difference. To make their life count for something bigger than themselves. To make more than a big splash.

This book is about helping you change the course of history one person at a time. If you're a coach, one player at a time. If you're a teacher or youth pastor, one student at a time. If you are a parent, one child at a time. If you're a leader, one team member at a time. These principles can help you *Ignite Future* and change the course of history, one person at a time!

24

Chapter 1

PRIMITIVE CONFIDENCE

What They Really Need First

As a clueless new dad, it didn't take long to have the shoulders of about every shirt I owned christened with smelly little white stains. Wanting to be an engaged, supportive husband, I helped out as much as I could with feeding time.

Our first born, was a cheerful little guy who could not hold his milk down, so we spent a lot of money providing Hunter with only the finest name brand formula. By the end of what seemed like every bottle, he would toss a small sample of his milk and cookies on my shoulder. My wife, Kirsten, and I figured this was just normal for babies (she was also much better at protecting her wardrobe with those little white appropriately named "burp-cloths"). After six months of this routine, our pediatrician suggested we try another formula to see if Hunter had a milk allergy.

Two kids later, my confidence at feeding time had improved dramatically. Not many new dads know anything about milk allergies and baby spit-up. All too often *you don't know what you don't know*. What I needed first was a good online tutorial on effective bottle feeding. What Hunter needed first was a tasty bottle of formula (which sounds like an oxymoron) that he could keep down.

When it comes to coaching, mentoring, or parenting, we often don't understand what people need first. Primitive confidence is one of those things they really do need first. Its presence is essential if they are going to thrive.

What Is Primitive Confidence?

Primitive confidence develops as a result of becoming skilled at something specific. It is an incredibly potent by-product of personal achievement. It has nothing to do with cockiness, arrogance, or high ego. This assurance flows from discovering basic competence in certain areas. It is a quiet confidence, a concrete belief in your ability to accomplish specific things well. It is the confidence to stick your neck out – like an increased risk-capacity – and try something new because of similar past success. This foundational layer of confidence is rooted in reality and is directly related to attaining a high level of skill in at least one specific area. It may also be something you are not even aware you possess. You simply gravitate to certain circumstance or opportunities. It is the ability to get good at one thing and to have benchmarks – measurements or reference points – that confirm your skills are real. Some of those benchmarks are obvious. *You* are actually playing first-string. *You* did make all-league, all-conference this year. *You* are first chair and *your* band did win the state championship. Other benchmarks may be subtler, a genuinely affirming word from a coach, band instructor, or a fellow player.

A child who begins to excel at something develops what cognitive psychologists call "self-efficacy." This is a form of self-confidence, a personal belief about your ability to accomplish certain tasks well. It's worth noting that "con-fidence" is equivalent to "with-faith;" a state in which the person steps into the unknown or unfamiliar with the growing knowledge that they have managed such challenges in the past. Perceived self-efficacy is concerned not with the number of skills you have, but with what you believe you can do with what you have.[11]

You can gain self-efficacy in almost any meaningful pursuit – such as a teacher, musician, quarterback, or coach. However, I interviewed leaders who were building more than simple self-efficacy. It was more like self-efficacy-*plus*. These high impact people had established foundational layers of confidence that extended well beyond the borders of their early talents, skills, and achievements. That complex foundation gave them a platform of confidence to take risks and launch into other pursuits where they found they could also excel. This in turn allowed them to not only overcome the fear of failure but also real failures along the way.

Where Do You Get It?
Most layers of primitive confidence are nurtured during high school and college, though the seeds are planted much earlier. Everyone I interviewed had at least one primitive confidence building experience by the time they reached high school, and eighty percent had two or more.[12]

For these leaders, primitive confidence had formed in four prominent places: on the job, on the team, in the band, and in competitive speech and debate. These four venues provided the optimal environment for this confidence to flourish. While these four activities were not exclusive, they were the top locations where primitive confidence developed in my initial research.

#1: On the Job
The biggest surprise during my interviews was discovering that the greatest venue for building

primitive confidence was on the job. Story after story revealed that first part-time jobs held incredible influence for gaining confidence. Lessons learned on the job were deeply experienced and left indelible marks. Most of these jobs were pursued by each person sensing the need to earn money. They weren't coerced by parents.If you have ever coached or taught teenagers, you know that part-time jobs often seem to be a distraction. But major formative work happens while flipping burgers or dragging a lawnmower around the neighborhood making door-to-door sales calls. Learning the value and reward of showing up on time, seeing firsthand what you can accomplish when you work hard at something, and figuring out how to get along with bosses and co-workers has lifelong influence.

Accepting responsibility on the job is an additional opportunity to grow and gain confidence. At home, mom and dad may expect certain tasks to be done, like mowing the lawn or feeding the dog, but being given responsibility by adults in a business setting can have a greater level of magnitude. Taking that responsibility and handling it well is incredibly formative.

Working the register at a Hardee's fast food built primitive confidence in one leader from the Pacific Northwest. "I was a good cashier," recalled Clark Tanner, former senior pastor of Beaverton Christian Church, "and I never touched a hamburger. I never worked the line, but I was fast and I connected with the customers."

He went on to describe how that confidence was refined: "When you work at a hamburger place like that, the people who come in generally order the same thing. Day after day, they never change. I would see people pull into the parking lot and I would get their order ready. As soon as they got to the counter it was there for them. I actually had people lined up just to get in my line because they knew that their order would be ready and waiting for them."

Other factors affirmed Clark's confidence. He noted, "The manager of the store told me, 'You are the only person I have ever left on cashier for a long period of time. After a while, a lot of people begin to take money out of the till, but I knew I could trust you. I watched you, and had no reservation about leaving you on the register.'"[13]

Clark Tanner excelled at taking care of customers. He delivered a superior level of service and was recognized for his skill, which helped to forge early layers of primitive confidence.

#2: On the Team

Team sports like football and basketball provided the second most influential venue to build primitive confidence. On the team, you honed athletic skills and became first-string. Since I had experienced this myself when I played high school football, this venue didn't come as a surprise. Individual sports like swimming or the martial arts also help confidence grow, but team sports provide the second most influential setting to get really good at something. The group aspects bring out individual strengths and unique abilities which are not as easy to identify in individual sports.

A team sports late-bloomer, I started playing high school football as a sophomore and proceeded to warm the bench. After the season ended something inside me clicked. I loved the game, but didn't like sitting on the bench and needed to improve, so I began my new weightlifting, running, and protein shake (steroid-free of course) regimen. Though pretty much still warming the bench, I got to see a bit more time on the field my junior year. By senior year, I found myself playing first-string offensive guard, with a fresh new layer of primitive confidence.

Everyone on the team benefits from the momentum that comes with a winning season. Football was colossal in molding primitive confidence in Joel Hunter, the leader of the highly innovative Northland Church in Central Florida. "I had three coaches who took me under their wing during my high school football career," he recalled:

"Our team was so good at what we did and that really inspired me to excel. I weighed 145 pounds and played on the line, so you can imagine how little that team was. We were the smallest kids in the league, but we went undefeated.

We were winning season after season, championship after championship, and it was because of our coaches who totally invested in us. They taught us discipline and how to think, as well as how to use our speed. There is no way we should have won the number of games we did, but they pulled more out of us than anybody possibly could have."[14]

Being part of a team teaches the importance of working with others, but it also offers the chance for each player to develop skills and excel. Dedicated athletes develop a strong work ethic by coming to practice, working out in the off-season, and attending sports camps and clinics. In addition to honing athletic skills, team sports allow hard working players the opportunity to rise to the top and become a first-string quarterback, all-league point guard or starting shortstop. Similarly, Angela Duckworth in her highly motivational book, *Grit*, says "What we have tended to find is that all that energy, drive, and commitment – all that grit – that was developed through athletics can almost always be transferred to something else."[15]

#3: In the Band

One influential leader of one of the largest churches in the US, recounted how being the drummer in a high school garage band that won the

"Battle of the Bands" in Detroit was a huge boost to his confidence.[16]

The performing arts are an excellent venue for attaining a high level of competence. Musicians, singers, dancers or actors can also compare their performance to their peers to see or hear how well they are doing, which can provide additional motivation to excel.

Among those I interviewed, marching bands, orchestras, church choirs, and even garage bands proved to be especially formative in building primitive confidence.

Former British Prime Minister Margaret Thatcher acknowledged the shaping influence performing arts had in her early years. "We were a musical family," she recalled. "From the age of five my parents had me learn the piano and my mother played too. In fact, I turned out to be quite good. I was fortunate enough to have excellent teachers and won several prizes at local music festivals."[17]

Ken Fong, an innovative pastor from Los Angeles spelled this out well. He said, "Music was my thing because it worked well for me and I kind of got my kudos there. Everybody's got to make it in something and that's kind of where I made it."[18]

Michael Foss, a gifted communicator and pastor of one of the largest Lutheran Churches in the Mid-West, recalled playing the lead role in the school play, saying "It was the first smash success of the drama department and was held over – that gave me great confidence."[19]

#4: In Competitive Speech & Debate

Though public speaking is considered one of the greatest fears of adults, the speech and debate team was the fourth most common venue to gain primitive confidence. Studying, preparing, practicing, and sharpening the ability to think quickly under pressure was incredibly influential for many. Venturing into this area sets you apart from most other people who avoid that kind of exposure.

Michael Foss recalled, "I was in high school speech and debate and found that I loved extemporaneous speaking. I think the confidence that I developed on the stage naturally carried over to my future career."[20] While not conscious of it at the time, this experience became for him a solid layer of primitive confidence.

How Do You Get It?

Though not exclusive, these four venues provide a context, a kind of human performance laboratory, to build a high level of skill. "When kids are playing sports or music or rehearsing for the school play, they are both challenged and having fun. There's no other experience in the lives of young people that reliably provides this combination of challenge and intrinsic motivation... There are countless research studies showing that kids who are more involved in extracurricular activities fare better on just about every conceivable metric – they earn better grades, have higher self-esteem, are less likely to get in trouble and so forth."[21]

In order to attain an expert level of performance, one famous study found that it takes between ten and twenty thousand hours of focused, deliberate practice.[22] Now, those I interviewed were not necessarily "expert" part-time employees, basketball players, musicians, or debate team members, but in the pursuit of excellence, very specific character qualities began to take shape and centered around four essential traits. These four reinforcing factors (RF) were pivotal in getting good at something and instrumental in forging foundational layers of primitive confidence.

Think about your own experiences growing up. Not everyone who worked with you at Taco Bell or

Starbucks, nor everyone on your baseball team or cheer squad, developed primitive confidence or lived a life of high impact.

To get really good at something and gain a layer of primitive confidence, you need four RF's working together to help you excel and sharpen your skills on the job, on the team, in the band, or during the debate season. What do those RF's look like?

Four Reinforcing Factors

#1. Reliability, *Not* Inconsistency

The first RF is reliability, *not* inconsistency. Reliability is the demonstrated capacity to be counted on by others to complete a job, a task, or a project by doing what you say you will do and not letting other people down.

Reliability also means being on time and requires honesty in the use of your time and the handling of money – especially other people's money.

So, as they grow up, how do kids acquire this trait? The seeds of reliability are most often planted at home, but sprout and grow up someplace else. A mom or dad's consistency – sometimes in working two or three jobs to pay the bills – and their example of what a reliable person is like can make big impressions on a child. Kids will imitate both good and bad parental habits.

What begins at home gets refined in other places, often under the watch of a boss, coach, or teacher.

Clark Tanner recalled an experience that affirmed and helped to cement his reliability, his ability to be trusted with great responsibility. The town where he grew up had only one cafeteria to serve all the schools and it was located at the elementary school. As a junior in high school, the principal asked him to drive one of those buses of fellow high school students over to the cafeteria for lunch each day. It was huge boost to his confidence to be trusted and relied upon at such a young age for that kind of responsibility.[23]

It would be great if you could just spray reliability on your kids like a squirt bottle, but they actually become more reliable collaterally. They learn it as a side benefit on the job, when they show up on time, punch the clock, and do their work. They get it by doing their homework without being reminded. They pick it up in sports, by coming to practice on time, working hard, and doing their part. They learn it in the performing arts, by coming to rehearsal on time and working as an ensemble. These contexts provide the backdrop for reliability to become a reality.

At home, parents can begin to lay a foundation for this by having consistent and reliable rules, schedules, and expectations for homework, free time, chores, and bedtime. Also key is being consistent in rewarding positive behaviors or giving consequences for negative behaviors. Too often parents can gravitate to primarily catching their kids doing something wrong; kids need someone spotting and highlighting what they do right. Parents can also be positive models for reliability and consistency by arriving on time for school, church, and community activities.

#2. Priority-Driven, *Not* Impulse Driven

The second RF is becoming more priority-driven, *not* impulse driven. This is the ability to say "yes" to what is important and "no" to what is not.

Even now as you read this you may be thinking, *"Is this a good time for a little snack? I can finish reading this later. What do we have in the refrigerator that sounds good?"*

Being priority-driven means taking the initiative to do what needs to be done regardless of any outside pressure or internal emotions. It is the ability to stay focused on a task at hand, in spite of distractions, impulses, and temptations.

Being driven by the right priorities is very similar to having self-discipline. Self-discipline affords a person the inclination to concentrate on a task as long as is necessary to learn, perfect, or complete it.

Just as with reliability, the priority-driven seeds start to grow in the home. According to Bob Russell, senior pastor emeritus of Southeast Christian Church in Louisville, Kentucky, "the discipline that you establish early stays with you the rest of your life."[24]

One recent study found that self-discipline is a better measure for predicting academic achievement than IQ. "We suggest another reason for students falling short of their intellectual potential: their failure to exercise self-discipline....We believe that many of America's children have trouble making choices that require them to sacrifice short-term pleasure for long-term gain, and that programs that build self-discipline may be the royal road to building academic achievement."[25]

How do kids become more priority-driven, more disciplined? These traits most often come as a by-product of other pursuits. When children (or adults) are engaged in, and enjoying a new interest like basketball or learning a new computer program, they spend a lot of time on the court or in front of a keyboard. That focused time begins to build skills and reinforces a cycle of self-discipline, driven by internal priorities not by impulses.

One such beneficial pursuit is learning to play an instrument. There are three distinct stages that help shape this learning process.

First, *forced practice* on a continuing basis is required – "You will practice your tuba before playing on the computer." Practicing regularly and making that a priority over other activities like social media or playing video games is key to instilling self-discipline.

Second, *assisted practice* with others builds confidence. Playing in a band reinforces the value of the hours spent practicing and allows musicians to compare their progress to others, as well as receive encouragement and praise from fellow band members.

Finally, *playing alone* shows the internal motivation of the true musician, who actually enjoys picking up the instrument to practice or play alone. Some young musicians never make it to this third stage, but looking back years later, many recognize the self-discipline that resulted from the first two stages.

#3. Hard Work, *Not* Natural Talent

The third RF is about learning what can be accomplished through hard work. It's not about innate talent, IQ, or any sort of coolness factor. It's perspiration that makes the difference.

One senior pastor at a large Presbyterian church in Northern California shared with me, "I learned from football that if you wanted to win you had to put in the effort. You had to be committed. One of the reasons we won is because we did it all year round."[26]

Proverbs 14:23 says: "All hard work brings a profit, but mere talk leads only to poverty." Learning the lesson of what hard work can accomplish builds a reservoir of confidence for future goals yet to be pursued.

Educators call this the Theory of Malleable Intelligence, or a Growth Mindset. Superior students believe they can change, improve, and become more intelligent by working hard. As a result, they aren't limited by perceived natural talents or genetic factors.

Nothing is more discouraging to a teacher than to see students with incredible potential quit trying because they believe they are just not smart enough. Somewhere between fourth grade and middle school, I came to the conclusion that I was not good at English grammar -- that I had no natural talent for the nuances of the King's English. Whenever classroom

36

discussions turned to the finer points of sentence diagrams, my eyes glazed over, I turned the volume down, and tuned out the opportunity to learn.

This deficit was confirmed during my first semester of college. Two pages into the required English entrance exam I knew I was doomed. I closed my test packet and signed up for remedial English (which essentially covered fourth grade through seventh grade English).

Surprisingly, in this self-paced remedial class, I worked hard, learned the material, and got an 'A'. After that glorious victory, I completed all the requisite English courses for my degree and have since learned three foreign languages. My hard work ethic prevailed over my obvious lack of natural talent.

This is not to say natural talents are not influential. They most definitely are, but when compared with a belief in the ability to improve through hard work, natural talents lose hands down. Multiple studies soundly reinforce this idea.[27] One need look no further than the world of sports to see recurring examples of hard work triumphing over talent – something that occurs often enough to show that it's not an anomaly.

One major study of sixth graders moving into seventh grade[28] found that high achieving sixth grade students who believed that intelligence (unchangeable natural intelligence, or talent) is fixed – that people are essentially born smart or not-so-smart – did poorly on achievement tests in seventh grade. Another group with a different belief about intelligence – that individuals can improve their intelligence by working hard or trying new strategies – did well on seventh grade achievement tests.

Interestingly, this second group included two groups of sixth graders. One group did well on sixth grade achievement tests and the other did poorly in sixth grade. However, both of these groups, who believed that with hard work and good strategies they could improve, did well on seventh grade achievement tests. So what a person believes about their ability to change or improve does make a big difference.

Well known author, John Irving, said "One reason I have confidence in writing the kind of novels I write, is that I have confidence in my stamina to go over something again and again no matter how difficult it is."[29] Regarding his own talent versus his work ethic, actor Will Smith said "I've never really viewed myself as particularly talented, where I excel is a ridiculous, sickening work ethic."[30]

Former Secretary of State and Chairman of the Joint Chiefs of Staff, Colin Powell, experienced the benefits of hard work one summer at a Pepsi bottling plant. Before he headed back to school for the fall, Powell was pulled aside by his foreman, who told him what a great job he had done with a mop. His work ethic was so stellar, the foreman told him to come back next summer to his same job.

Powell counter-offered to come back and work, but on the bottling machine instead of behind a mop. That next summer his foreman gave him a spot on the bottling machine, and by the end of August, Powell was deputy shift leader. He explained how he learned such a valuable lesson in hard work by believing: "All work is honorable. Always do your best, because someone is watching."[31]

How is a hard work mindset developed? One way is to start and finish small projects successfully. It's critical for kids to see what can be achieved by the end of the day through consistent effort and staying on task. Parents, teachers, and mentors can play a key role in fostering a hard work mindset by the example they set.

I vividly remember the summer weekend my dad and I built a new brick patio. He was no brick mason (and to my knowledge never made anything else out of brick). Going to the brickyard, we loaded up the back of our station wagon with bricks, bags of sand, and then drove home. After hauling it all to the backyard, we dug out a big patch of the grass, built a border out of two by fours, then spread out and leveled the sand base. We laid down the bricks and cut some to fit using a hammer and mason's chisel, tapping the last ones into place with a rubber mallet. From then on we used that patio all the time, and that weekend project etched a powerful picture in my mind – a picture of what I could achieve when I put my shoulder into it.

From an academic angle, I remember how a massive high school term paper project reinforced my beliefs about my potential to do well in the classroom. I chose to do a history of the modern golf ball (you must be wondering where you can get a copy of this riveting work)! Though I've never been accused of being the brightest light on the Christmas tree, I learned that working hard, finishing the paper, and getting an A+ (very rare for me) bolstered my belief that if I put enough effort into a school project I could do it.

Duckworth describes an interesting formula that reinforces this idea of hard work and effort. "Talent is how quickly your skills improve when you invest effort. Achievement is what happens when you take your acquired skills and use them. Talent x effort=skill, and Skill x effort=achievement.... ...Effort factors into calculations twice, not once. Effort builds skill. At the very same time, effort makes skill productive."[32]

This RF is not about talent, it's about horsepower and hard work. It's about applying consistent effort to a task, then seeing what can be accomplished by going all out to get the job done.

#4. Teamwork, *Not* Ball Hogging

This fourth RF is all about teamwork, *not* ball-hogging. Teamwork is learning how each player has a unique role to play, and how all players can best work together as one unified force.

The success of a team hinges on the selfless and collective efforts of individuals. When people are doing what they are good at, alongside others doing what they are good at, the net results can be exponentially better. The whole is truly greater than the sum of the parts, but not everyone who plays on a team learns this.

My daughter played on the same soccer team for four years in a row. The first couple of years, these first and second grade girls would clump together around the ball like high-energy puppies in need of A.D.D. meds. Inevitably, one of the girls in the pack would break loose, kick the ball down the field, and shoot. Repeat that multiple times and you have a pretty good idea of how the game and the season went.

Now move up the calendar to fourth grade. We had the same girls, the same coach and the same parents cheering and screaming on the sidelines, but something was different. The girls actually started passing the ball to each other as they ran down the field, and the player closest to the goal would shoot.

I couldn't believe what I was seeing! The girls were playing as a team. It was a major paradigm shift in their youth soccer world. They were somehow becoming conscious of the fact that by passing the ball to their teammates they would score more points and win more games by playing as a team.

The core lessons in teamwork are learned on the field or on the court, not from a book, seminar, or class – but by playing on a team. However, not everyone who plays learns the value of teamwork. It takes a deeper level of insight. Teamwork lessons are often recognized and reinforced by looking in the rearview mirror, reflecting back on childhood experiences of being part of a team.

As a parental veteran of youth sports (though I still don't understand soccer rules), I have watched some coaches quickly figure out which nine-year-olds are the most talented and let those select few hog the ball for entire games, while other coaches assess player skills and work aggressively with their whole team to help them play together and win as a team. The players on the latter coach's teams are much more likely to learn the lessons of team work, that it's not about the individual talent, accolades, and success, it's about both winning and losing *as a team*.

So, in review...

Four Reinforcing Factors To High Achievement:

#1. Reliability, *Not* Inconsistency:
Making good on personal commitments.

#2. Priority-Driven, *Not* Impulse Driven:
Doing what needs to get done.

#3. Hard Work, *Not* Natural Talent:
Knowing hard work pays off.

#4. Teamwork, *Not* Ball Hogging:
*Seeing the value of people with unique strengths
working together as one team.*

To Conclude
What if I didn't get primitive confidence? Is it ever too late? It is never too late to get really good at something

- especially when you have a genuinely strong interest in it. Whether a sport, hobby, performing art, or a work-related skill like public speaking, you can develop expertise. Expertise, or getting really good at something, provides the foundation for primitive confidence. Gaining expertise is not simply about logging thousands of hours of practice. It's about putting in "deliberate practice."[33] Finding an area of interest then throwing yourself into focused, deliberate practice, is key. Duckworth notes four components of deliberate practice: "One, a clearly defined stretch goal. Two, full concentration and effort. Three, immediate and informative feedback. Four, repetition with reflection and refinement."[34]

Years ago I worked as a ship renovation consultant for the Navy. On my first day on the job I was given an official sticker for my windshield that would allow me to enter the 32nd Street Naval Base in San Diego.

Every day I would come to work and drive up to the gate. The guard on duty would salute and I would drive right on through, like clockwork. Eventually, that sticker gave me the unconscious confidence that I could drive right on base any time I wanted.

A decade later, as an architect, I was working on renovation projects at McClellan Air Force Base in Sacramento, but I no longer had an official sticker for easy access. Whenever I had a meeting on base or needed to get to the jobsite, I had to stop at the main gate, give my name, show my driver's license and my business card, then wait as the guard on duty checked "the list" to see if I was pre-approved to enter that day.

It was a royal pain. Some days entering the base was no problem and I would even get a salute. Other days, I was "Mr. No-name-on-the-list" and the guard had to get on the phone to find someone who could vouch for me. Needless to say, I had no confidence of getting on that base. Every time I drove up to the gate I wondered if I had made "the list."

Primitive confidence is like having an official sticker to get you where you need to go. You may not even be aware that you have it, but you experience its benefits daily.

Personal Reflection...

1. As you look back, what were some of the most formative experiences from your childhood and teenage years?

2. What was it about those experiences that made them so influential?

3. What did you get really good at as a child or teenager? Did you work to develop that skill or did it come naturally? Is there an ability you would have liked to develop?

4. As you think about your first part-time job(s) as a teenager or young adult, what influential lessons can you recall learning?

5. Do you think of yourself as a reliable person? Why or why not?

6. Do you tend to be driven more by your priorities or your impulses? Would others say you are a disciplined person?

7. Have you ever been told you are industrious or a hard worker? Why is that?

8. What is one goal you have worked hard to achieve? What did it feel like to finally accomplish your goal?

9. Can you recall a time when you experienced someone "hogging the ball" either literally or figuratively? What affect did this have on you personally?

10. What are some of the enduring lessons you have learned from being on a team?

11. Do you feel you gained a layer of primitive confidence as a teenager or young adult? Why or why not?

12. If not, what could you begin to do today to work towards getting really good at one thing?

Igniting Future
When you think about others you are investing in...

1. Have you taken the time to explore by observation or conversation whether they have areas of primitive confidence? What have you discovered?

2. Are they developing primitive confidence? If so, in what areas?

3. What kinds of extra-curricular pursuits are they committed to? Are they doing well and developing a higher level of skill?

4. What can you do to help deepen their skills?

5. If they don't have any extra-curricular interests, is there a particular sport, hobby, or the performing arts area you could help them pursue? (It is never too late to encourage this, --particularly an activity that involves a team or group of peers.)

6. What can you begin doing to encourage this?

7. How reliable would you consider them to be? (high, medium, low)

8. What kind of incremental new responsibilities could you delegate to them to help expand the level of their reliability?

9. What positive incentives can you begin providing to encourage those new responsibilities?

10. How priority driven would you consider them to be? (high, medium, low)

11. Are there rewards you can put in place that foster self-discipline and discourage impulsiveness?

12. Do they tend to rely more on their natural talents or their level of effort to complete homework, other projects, or assignments?

13. Is there a small project where you could enlist their help to complete it?

14. What kinds of regular chores, classroom duties, or team projects can you assign them?

Chapter 2

VICARIOUS CONFIDENCE

Discovering the Magnitude of Your Influence

Why does it always seem that the tool you desperately need in a crisis is the one your kids most recently converted into a sandbox toy? Over the years I've had to buy more replacement screwdrivers, pliers, measuring tapes, and chisels than I'd like to admit.

My daughter Hannah and youngest son Hudson loved to build... anything. They liked to use my tools and were not afraid to tackle an unapproved demolition or construction project. I've found more than one rusted set of pliers or wire-cutters in the bushes, flowerbeds, or tree house. In my lost tool recovery rants I often threaten to put a lock on my tool chest, but I always relent.

I actually decided years ago that I would rather let them have access to my tools and risk a few lost to the sandbox than have a pristine, fully-stocked workbench. My children's fondness for building and tinkering with stuff didn't come out of the blue. They picked it up from helping me put in ceiling fans, install new doors, or replace dry-rotted decking. In the midst of these home improvement adventures I think they acquired more than just a knack for building. They were gaining vicarious confidence.

What Is Vicarious Confidence?

The magnitude of a parent's or mentor's influence is rarely seen in real time. Most often, when we do see it, it is in retrospect looking back over the years.

Vicarious confidence is something you receive from others. It is a layer of confidence instilled from a distance, imparted from one person to another. Vicarious confidence allows you to accomplish something you wouldn't normally be able to on your own, without any previous experience.

How Do You Get It?

Virtually all the leaders I interviewed had at least one person they could point to who dramatically shaped their growth and personal confidence. Frequently they credited more than one influential parent, teacher, coach, or boss with instilling confidence vicariously.

In describing *how* these adults made a difference in their lives, literally everyone recounted at least one of three ways that those unofficial mentors inspired vicarious confidence – through role-modeling and example; by affirming genuine talents and skills; and by pushing them into over-their-head stretching opportunities where they had to grow in order to survive.

There are times mentors intentionally act as role models, saying "do it like this." Other times, people of influence passively and unknowingly inspire confidence in others. Whether the guidance given is active or passive, the net result is vicarious confidence.

The First Way... By Example
(Show Me How It's Done)

The first path to gaining vicarious confidence appears when influential people are living examples. Just watching a history teacher's passion or a coach's commanding presence can impart vicarious confidence.

Nelson Mandela's father died when he was only nine years old. A tribal chieftain named Jongintaba took the young boy in and cared for him. This man had a powerful influence on Mandela's yet-to-be-formed leadership style.

In *Nelson Mandela, A Biography*, author Martin Meredith describes this effect: "At tribal meetings at the Great Palace, when high-ranking counselors gathered to discuss both local and national issues, he (young Mandela), observed how Jongintaba would take care to hear all opinions, listening in silence to whatever criticism was made, even of himself, before making a summary of what had been said and endeavoring to find a consensus of views. It was a style of leadership which made a profound impression upon him."[35]

Now, watching how Mandela has handled himself in the face of tremendous adversity, it is easy to see how Jongitaba vicariously rubbed off on him.

The power of a role model is colossal and starts to work on us before we know it's actually happening. We find ourselves using words, phrases, or gestures of people we admire, respect, or even find entertaining, without knowing we are doing it. Think of some of the common phrases you use -- most likely you picked up certain words or expressions without much conscious thought from your mom or dad, an older sibling, a former boss, teacher, youth leader, or coach.

One key factor in role modeling is that the person setting the example must have more advanced skills and abilities than the fledgling. The exemplar needs to be ahead in terms of skills or wisdom, but not too far ahead. If someone is perceived as too far ahead, or not even in the same league, it will not inspire as much *'I can do that too'* kind of confidence.

One Friday night, a group of friends and I went climbing at an indoor rock-climbing center. Some of us had recent climbing experience, some had ancient experience (that would be me), and some had no experience. A couple of our best climbers did the belaying – holding onto the ropes – for the rest of us.

After we all had the chance to do a few twenty to thirty-foot climbs, one of my friends attempted a more challenging ascent. To reach the top, he had to use a *chimney move* for the last eight feet, which had no artificial hand or foot holds on the climbing surface, but had two opposing rock faces about four feet apart. With some scowling, grunting, and perseverance, he made it to the top.

As I watched this I said to myself, "If he can do it, I can do it." He was in better shape than I was, but not by much. I went next and after a few grunts and scowls I made it. Now if a resident rock-star climber had done that same climb and chimney move before I did, it would *not* have produced the same level of vicarious confidence as when my buddy did it. Duckworth similarly notes that "Because one thing that makes you better at basketball is playing with kids who were just a little more skilled. Flynn called this virtuous cycle of skill improvement the social multiplier effect..."[36] The most effective examples need to be ahead of us, *but not too far out in front*, or they can actually de-motivate us.

Bosses and supervisors can be excellent suppliers of vicarious confidence. Their workplace stories act as substitutes for first-hand, on-location leadership experience. Their war stories describing mistakes and successes can vicariously replace actual work experiences we may have missed along our own career trajectories – or that we have yet to experience if we're just starting out. Careers aren't long enough to do everything and vicarious experience sometimes fills the gap.[37]

Ray Takata was one of the most competent architects I've ever known. He hired me right out of college to work as a project architect in his firm. Ray was a master at telling his own war stories to inspire vicarious confidence.

One afternoon, I stepped into his office to confess that I had just messed up on some construction details I had drawn for a school auditorium project. Out of his own pocket, the contractor was going to have to pay to fix my mistake and I felt like a dog.

Ray barely took a breath as he began telling me about the time he drew the plans for a large college locker room remodel. He said that when he was writing the specifications for the ceramic tile, he wrote the wrong color number and the contractor ended up installing pink tile in the men's showers. His boss at the time had to pay for the tile to be torn out and replaced. After that, Ray never said another word about my detail incident. He didn't need to.

The power of good role models to inspire and instruct is nothing new. During the time of the Roman Empire, around A.D. 65, one of the best examples of someone imparting vicarious confidence to another comes from Paul the Apostle. He had been mentoring a young leader named Timothy who was struggling with leadership confidence issues. In I Timothy 4:12, Paul wrote to him, "*Don't let anyone think less of you because you are young. Be an example to all believers in what you say, in the way you live, in your love, your faith, and your purity.*"[38]

That phrase he used, *be an example,* is a translation of the ancient Greek word *Tupos,* which literally meant a blow of a hammer that is used to chisel an image or statue. It was used figuratively for modeling ethical behavior.[39] Paul was urging Timothy to be the model, in spite of his young age.

Ray Johnston, senior pastor of Bayside Church in Northern California, had an incredibly influential youth pastor as a role model when he was starting out in ministry:

> Just watching our high school pastor Chuck Miller, from Lake Avenue Congregational Church was huge. It was just sheer watching. – I was in this guy's ministry for five years and it is still the best youth ministry I have ever seen. He is an amazing guy. He was like the General Patton of youth ministry. I just watched him, --a great up front communicator, watching what he did, and then going out and pretty much doing what he did. I was on their youth staff and I was able to see things up close. I'd watch him develop staff and watch him speak. For me, easily, there is nothing else that comes close to his example.[40]

The Second Way... **By Affirmation (Tell Me I Can Do It)**

The second path to vicarious confidence appears when people you respect affirm your talents and worth. What is critical is that your talent must be real and connected to something specific, where you actually performed at a high level. It can't be inflated praise like Homer Simpson telling Bart that someday he'll play for the Green Bay Packers. It must be real and based on actual facts.

Kenneth Ulmer grew up in East Saint Louis, Illinois. He started his career in broadcasting, and then went into sales before becoming a pastor. Under his leadership, Faithful Central Bible Church in Los Angeles mushroomed in size and eventually purchased the former home of the Los Angeles Lakers, The Forum.[41]

When I asked him who had a big influence on him in his early years, he told me about two teachers. "My high school was predominantly a white school," he said. "My English teacher was a lady named Miss Mildred Rongey. One day Miss Rongey told me 'Kenneth, you can go as far as you can dream.' "[42]He also mentioned another memorable teacher who influenced him. "Mrs. Triplett was my 7th grade English teacher and had the strangest perfume I ever smelled," he recalled. "It would make your nose burn.

"She was the first black person I'd ever met who traveled abroad. Every summer she would travel out of the country and at the beginning of the school year she would bring in all these pictures of where she had gone. She brought pictures of the Eiffel Tower and everyone would ooh and ah. She said to me 'Kenneth, one day you're going there. The world is bigger than East Saint Louis!' "[43] These well-respected teachers instilled vicarious confidence through their words of affirmation.

In her memoir, *Tough Choices*, Former Hewlett Packard CEO, Carly Fiorina shares a great example of affirmation, "For whatever reason, the dean of the business school, Dr. Rudy Lamone, saw something in me... He asked for my help in devising a more effective alumni program. I was amazed. Whatever did I know about such a thing? He gave me an opportunity to work with him; and learn from him; and most important, be taken seriously by him. He treated me as an adult and a peer. He thought I had potential and wanted to help me explore it... It was a simple thing that he did, and yet it made all the difference for me."[44]

During my interview with Raul Reis, senior pastor of Calvary Chapel Golden Springs in Southern California, he talked about the confidence he gained by the example and the affirmation of his Kung Fu instructor, Jimmy Wu:

Jimmy Wu influenced me, not only like a father, but he showed me that I could be the best in what I was doing. He coached me and discipled me in the martial arts. He used me in every Kung Fu demonstration. Even today, forty years later, I'm still teaching and I'm feeling now all of the lessons and everything he gave me. He's the one who made me who I am today in the martial arts.

I also gained confidence in how to get along with people and how to talk to people. Because we had to do demonstrations where you're facing two to three thousand people, so you're nervous. But by watching him—even though he couldn't speak good English—the confidence that he had being in front of an audience and presenting himself as a martial arts teacher was huge.[45]

Another important aspect is how the person giving affirmation is viewed by the one receiving it. It's one thing for a total stranger to tell you that you have great talent, and quite another for a deeply respected parent, teacher, boss, or coach, to say the same thing with total sincerity. The encouragement you receive from a boss can also have a powerful emotional impact.[46] The affirmation from a supervisor you respect is far more influential than a boss who gives only technical advice or expertise.

Suppose someone tells you, "You should be an astronaut!" If you happen to be a student at the Air Force Academy graduating at the top of your class and the professor who says this to you is a former astronaut, then your vicarious confidence surges. If it's your Uncle Henry who says this while you're watching *Space Monkey* or *Apollo 13*, it probably won't have the same effect. When a person we perceive as respected and credible affirms our talents and worth,

56

then it usually results in a solid layer of vicarious confidence.

The Third Way... By A Push
(Push Me to Where I Can Grow)

The third path to vicarious confidence is revealed by a push, a little shove into what are often called "stretch assignments."[47] These are the times you get pushed into doing something outside your comfort zone, when you are challenged to learn new things, sometimes even for survival.

Imagine your football coach asking you to play defensive end for the first time when you have been a lineman your entire career. What happens? You work harder to get up to speed, to catch up and learn the new position. The net result with this push is that your confidence increases and you become a better player – not just at defensive end, but an all-around better and more versatile player.

The push can come from someone who is well known and well liked, or it can even come from someone you don't like. It could be a boss who gives you a new assignment way beyond normal expectations. It can be a push to enroll in a certain class from a professor who affirms your talent – a class you wouldn't have chosen on your own that turns out to be a milestone experience. It is the challenge before you, that gap between your previous experience and what you need now, that provides the motivational force in these push situations.[48]

When my oldest son Hunter turned twelve, one of his new chores became mowing the lawn. It didn't take him long to master mowing our microscopic plot of grass in California with our non-motorized push-mower. Ever since he was a toddler he has never been fond of loud machinery, so I kept the weed-eater and power-blower work for myself.

But when we moved to the dairyland of Wisconsin, his lawn mowing duty expanded to half an acre. Now fourteen, he needed a push, an incentive to tackle this new territory. I knew he still didn't like loud noises, but we needed some power to cut this new farm-like expanse. So I pulled him into the search for a better mower and before we knew it we were driving home with a new self-propelled *Toro* mower. With his allowance now doubled and his confidence increased, he has never even flinched at the loud rattle of that new *Toro*.

To Conclude

Vicarious confidence is confidence instilled from a distance, from one person to another. It is imparted actively and passively along three paths: *By Example, By Affirmation, and By a Push*. It is built when people we respect are examples, give affirmation, and push us into places where we can grow.

This confidence is constructed in layers and varies over time. During high school it's inspired by coaches, teachers, and parents. In the college and post-college years, it comes from professors, youth leaders, and bosses. Most of us can think of at least one parent, teacher, or supervisor who saw our potential, pushed us, and challenged us to do things we would have never signed up for if left to ourselves. Layers of vicarious confidence continue to form throughout life. There is no age limit. Just an openness to receive it.

Mr. Fenwick, my seventh-grade woodshop teacher, was one of those who gave me a little push. I don't remember a lot about him, except for the fact that he was tall, lanky, and had a huge mustache. At the end of the school year he asked me if I would be his teacher's aide the next fall. I was no expert craftsman in the woodshop, but Mr. Fenwick asked me anyway.

That next year, not only did I get to have two periods of woodshop, but I was now the helper-dude, the go-to guy, when Mr. Fenwick was too busy. For most kids something like this may be no big deal, but for me it was huge. Prior to that, I didn't grow up experiencing what it was like to be the go-to guy, class leader, or the next Aaron Rodgers. I was the chubby kid whose mom had to buy him "husky-size" blue jeans.

When I got to middle school, I began to grow taller than wider (no more husky-size) and the timing of Mr. Fenwick's affirmation and push couldn't have been more pivotal. He gave me my first large dose of vicarious confidence.

By Example... *Show Me How It's Done*

By Affirmation... *Tell Me I Can Do It*

By a Push... *Push Me To Where I Can Grow*

Personal Reflection...

1. Who are the people that have made a lasting impact upon you during your teen, college, and post-college/early career years?

2. In what ways were they inspiring role models or examples to you?

3. Were you conscious of their impact at the time or was it years later looking back?

4. How did they affirm you? What kind of influence did their affirmation have on you?

5. Can you recall a time when you felt "pushed" into a "growing experience" by someone? How did you feel about it at the time?

6. Why do you feel this experience was so influential? What do you think might have happened if you had not been pushed?

Igniting Future
When you think about others you are investing in...

1. Are they developing vicarious confidence? Who has had or is having the greatest influence on them?

2. Who are the role models they look up to?

3. Who is affirming their strengths and abilities?

4. Are there things you can do to help facilitate more quality contact between your kids or students and these people?

5. Is there an area you could be a better role model for them? What steps can you take to improve your influence?

6. Can you think of something they can be "pushed" into that would stretch them? What do you need to do to set that up?

7. Are there people who are negative role models or influences in their lives? What can you constructively do to help minimize this?

Chapter 3

COMMAND CONFIDENCE

The Long-Lasting Benefit Of Leading Almost Anything

It's not often that I read the book after I've seen the movie, but in the case of the popular HBO World War II series *Band of Brothers*, that's exactly what I did. One aspect of the storyline gripped me the most. In the first episode, Easy Company started their initial training with Captain Herbert Sobel in command. He was a tyrant and demanded the respect of the soldiers under him solely based upon rank. However, very quickly on the battlefield, Lieutenant Dick Winters was asked to step up and take over the command from Sobel. Winters had earned the respect of the men of Easy Company and they served heroically under him throughout the rest of the war.[49] Winters brought with him many layers of Primitive Confidence from his earlier years. During his tour of duty in the European theatre, many new layers of *Command Confidence* were forged, that I believe, allowed him to flourish and become a man of great impact and influence. At the beginning of their training Captain Sobel was *in command*, but he never did develop or demonstrate *Command Confidence.*

What Is It?

This is the confidence you gain leading almost anything, when you are in charge and guiding others to reach a common goal, or achieve a common task. It's not about gaining a more imposing, or impressive title. It's about having responsibility for others and accomplishing your mission.

I got my first dose of command confidence my senior year of high school on Wednesday afternoons. My youth pastor, Bill Flanders, asked me to lead a Bible study with three guys. Rick, Tim, and Andy, -- all sophomores, who grew up going to church, knew all the Bible stories, and already memorized a boatload of Bible verses. I was a newcomer to church, God, and faith, but I was a senior and they weren't. I also had just done the same study with my youth pastor which gave me a brisk head start. The four of us met together for about six months, but leading that group changed the entire trajectory of my life. This was my first taste of leading something.

How Do You Get It?

Weight of Responsibility + Wins

Layers of command confidence are forged when you are leading others and the weight of responsibility is on your back. These layers don't come from simply leading, but leading *well*, having a "win", and receiving legitimate positive acknowledgment of your leadership performance. It is the "weight" plus the "win" that creates a game-changing combination.

The Weight

The weight of responsibility pressing in on you has an incredibly strong ability to shape your character and build layers of command confidence. When a youth pastor, a parent, or a teacher you respect is counting on you to lead a group of others, there is great motivational power to stay on task and do a good job. Just to be asked to lead something by someone you respect creates a positive momentum at the starting line. If you don't lead, there is a strong likelihood that the job won't get done, or done well. For example, if your sixth grade teacher has the whole class number-off, say, one to five, and then says "all the ones are the group leaders" it won't have the same force *as if she had picked you by name* and given you the weight of responsibility.

THE WEIGHT OF RESPONSIBILITY

The Wins

For a layer of command confidence to form, you need the weight of responsibility plus a "win". Even a "little win" can be enough. A win occurs when you successfully pull off what you were asked to lead. No one got hurt, no mutinous actions erupted from your team, you got the job done, and it turned out well. It doesn't have to be an A+ performance to count as a win. It just needs to have a positive outcome. Gaining momentum is the key. Little wins build positive upward momentum.

A "WIN"

On the flipside, when you're in charge of others with new responsibility, negative outcomes can have a disastrous effect on command confidence. Doing poorly with an early leadership responsibility can be exponentially negative. The resulting damaging inertia can be difficult to overcome.[50]

Back when dinosaurs were on the earth and I was a middle school ministry director at my church, I began to feel the weight of leadership responsibility on my shoulders. We had a midweek youth group gathering and once a month we would do a special event and encourage students to invite their friends. The night we loaded up every college age volunteer's car with students and headed up the 405 freeway to play mini-golf was a night to remember. The students had a blast and were definitely on the wild side. We caught one seventh grader teeing off his ball out onto the freeway. A record number of balls were lost in the water features throughout the course. The mini golf manager made sure to tell me that our youth group was not welcome back. But that was not the worst of it. I lost track of the time and it was a Wednesday night, a school night. Our caravan didn't roll back into the parking lot until after 10:00 PM. Parents were fuming as they had been waiting for over an hour to pick up their kids. This was clearly no smashing success for my command confidence. I felt the serious "weight" of responsibility, but definitely not the "win".

Months later, we loaded up the students for another special event, the "Day-After-The-July 4th Water Balloon Massacre." The fact that I was still in charge and allowed to even do another event with students is airtight evidence for the grace of God. We joined Chuck Swindoll's church at the time, EV Free Church of Fullerton, which had a much larger middle school group than ours. We showed up with 60 students and morphed in with their 200+ students and the water balloons were flying! It was a huge success. The students and volunteer staff had a blast and we got everyone back home on time. Parents were happy, students and staff were happy, and I experienced the "weight" of responsibility plus a "win". This soundly put the wind back into my sails for sure.

Where and When Do You Get It?

High School, College, Post-College Years

Since you need to be leading something to build command confidence, it doesn't fully form until high school, when leadership roles are more common. In my initial study of advanced leaders I found that:

- 80 percent of those interviewed reported building command confidence during high school
- 95 percent in the college years
- 100 percent during post-college years

During high school, the three most common places to develop command confidence are: #1, in a church youth group; #2, in a team sport like baseball, basketball, or football; and #3, in student government or campus clubs. These three venues were not the only places to get this, but were most common. It also doesn't mean command confidence can't form earlier, like in middle school, but the opportunities to lead at that age are much less.

During the High School Years
#1: Church Youth Group

A healthy church youth group is one of the most likely places to foster command confidence in the high school years. It happens before you know it when a youth pastor, or another adult leader, singles you out and asks you to help in the next big event, lead some kind of small group discussion or a missions trip team. It could come from leading worship, either solo or in a band. It's happens when you move across the line from attending the youth group to becoming responsible to help lead other students.

Once you're in a leadership role command confidence starts to form. Not just when you are in charge of something, but when you get positive feedback. A high-five from your leader, or a "good job!" from another student you respect can be all it takes. So many of us don't realize the expanded power our praise and affirmation has when developing other leaders. A smile, fist bump, or firm pat on the shoulder is all it may take to reinforce command confidence in an emerging student leader.

Often, the more subtle the praise you receive, the better impact it has. When a leader goes overboard and throws a huge party over something you did *fairly well* it sometimes comes across as forced or insincere. In the women's gymnastics competition in the 2012 summer Olympics you could feel the difference between genuine and disingenuous praise. When a US woman finished her event she walked off and received courtesy hugs from her teammates. For whatever reason, there was not much authentic emotion, and it came across as more obligatory. However, when the Russian gymnasts finished an event they were engulfed by hugs from teammates with honest tears and sincere emotion. You felt these Russian gymnasts were really happy at their teammate's success.

Like the affirmation of vicarious confidence, our affirmation to build command confidence has to be based on reality, where the young leader is doing good work. Genuine praise connected to a job well done creates positive memories that can last for decades.

#2: Team Captain

Building command confidence through sports takes more than just being on the team or the improved performance gained with primitive confidence. It takes holding a leadership position like team captain to forge this layer. When the weight of responsibility is pressing down on you, as your coach looks to you to set a positive example, as your team-mates look to you to take your job seriously, command confidence is born.

For Bob Russell, his role as quarterback and team captain was highly influential in building layers of command confidence.

> "I was asked to be the quarterback on our high school football team, and we had a really good team. The coach would entrust the quarterback, for the most part, for calling plays, and expect him to be a leader. As quarterback and co-captain of the football team, was my first big opportunity that I had of doing something where I was expected to lead and people followed. That was a real positive experience for me

#3: Student Government or Campus Club Leader

The third place this confidence was built is by leading others as a student body president, a cabinet member, or leading a campus group like 4H, yearbook staff, or the school newspaper. Planning big events, pulling them off, working to deadlines, getting along with people, and receiving positive feedback on your leadership made these roles a significant source of command confidence. You have a chance for 'weight' + 'wins'!

Pastor Ken Fong, reported the benefit of lessons learned on the student council. "Even in student council, you had to organize the junior-senior banquet. As small as that seems, it was very significant in cutting my teeth on what it meant to run a meeting and simply follow a project through to completion, and have to build consensus."[51] These measurable responsibilities were very positive in building command confidence. Command Confidence doesn't grow until someone puts a baton of responsibility in your hand and says, "Go!"

For Kenton Beshore, former senior pastor of Mariners Church in Southern California, his experience as school yearbook editor was a big command confidence builder. He recalled, "The only leadership position I really took in high school was the editor of the yearbook. That was because there was a real fascinating teacher and he just had me do it. I didn't go looking for it. It was just sort of given to me. This teacher just went, "You can do this." So, all of a sudden I'm the editor of the yearbook. That's probably why, I began to see I had the ability to lead. I was surprised by how many students would do things that I needed them to do and I could make it fun."[52]

During The College Years

In the college years command confidence is most likely to grow in two places, as a volunteer leader, or as a supervisor in a part-time job.

#1: Volunteer Positions

These volunteer positions are usually leadership roles in churches, student-focused ministries, fraternities, sororities, and campus clubs. They include multiple roles such as a small group leaders, worship leaders, or youth ministry intern or leader.

One influential volunteer position was held by Bishop Kenneth Ulmer as the social chairman in his fraternity. He said "The whole social calendar of the fraternity was on me. You learn planning techniques; you learn the challenge of working with people of different opinions... many times there was a great rivalry between some of the fraternities and sororities... I think you learn negotiation skills, communication skills, you learn compromise, you learn how to work with others, you learn how to affirm those with whom you may not even agree."[53]

Steve Stroope, Senior pastor of Lake Point Church, in the Dallas area, shared a valuable volunteer experience during his college years. "I'll tell you one thing that did have a big influence on me is my *Young*

Life experience. *Young Life* exposed me to the fact there were Christians in other denominations and it got me out of the closed system of my own denomination. It was a benchmarking experience that really broadened my horizons about how you do church government, how you do strategy for outreach, and how you do leadership. When you do *Young Life* and you've got 125 unchurched kids sitting there you learn how to be culturally relevant or you give up!"[54]

#2: Part-Time Jobs

Part-time jobs were influential in building command confidence as a result of having more responsibility, supervising and leading others. The part-time job could be almost any role that requires you to accept greater responsibility and supervise others. This is a major change. It's huge! It's like going from one side of the Grand Canyon to the other, or dishwasher to chef. Some people don't do well moving up the food chain and supervising others. They either aren't mature enough for it, or don't have the right personality and skills.

My friend, Bill Coyne, related how formative his first job was. He started working as a high school sophomore part-time at a Jewell Osco Drugstore and continued through his college years. He built his first layers of command confidence there on the job. Initially re-stocking merchandise, sweeping and mopping floors, then working the register, and helping out in the pharmacy, he eventually moved up to assistant manager while finishing his degree at the University of Illinois. He put in long hours, worked hard, functioned efficiently, and was rewarded for his hard work, creativity, and competence. After graduating from USC Law School and spending many years in a successful large law firm, he became CEO of Raley's Supermarket chain on the West Coast.[55]

During the Post-College Years... On the Job

In the post-college years and beyond, you build command confidence on-the-job. Having a variety of supervisory experiences managing others helps this to form. Workplace culture is another significant influence on building command confidence.

Four Influential Job Assignments

In one of the most comprehensive studies of how people of influence actually developed on-the-job, McCall, Lombardo and Morrison in their book *Lessons of Experience*, interviewed one hundred and ninety executives from six major corporations. During each interview they asked executives to identify key events that made a significant difference in the way they influence others.[56]

One reason new job assignments are so formative is largely due to being confronted with totally new situations that make your existing ways of doing things inadequate and force you to either grow and learn, or face-plant and tank.[57] Four formative types of job assignments rose to the top:

#1. Your First Supervisory Experience

Supervision forces you to learn that dealing with people is far different than having technical expertise. It's one thing to know how to repair a broken waterline. It's an entirely different set of skills needed to know how to manage the people who repair them.[58]

#2. Starting A New Department, Division, or Branch from scratch,

Leading a team that is starting a new venture can be incredibly formative. Lessons are learned at the speed of light, because with rapid change comes rapid growth. In these settings you learn how to organize, set priorities, and persevere during difficult situations. Also, you discover that leadership can be lonely.[59]

#3. Turning a division or department around, --a fix-it type assignment.

Being responsible for fixing a damaged or broken department or division, demands mental and relational toughness. In turn-around situations, those in charge learned how to be tough, how to be persuasive, and how to focus on results.[60]

#4. A major promotion or a large leap in the scope.

When your workplace scope of responsibility expands, it demands a new set of relational and leadership skills. The necessity of relying on other people, thinking big picture, and follow-through, were key lessons learned in these settings.[61] Learning these skills helps command confidence to form.

However, in some cases when the scope of one's responsibility expands too far, where there is too large of a leap in scope and you get promoted far above your current level of responsibility, there can be a significant failure at that new expanded level. The wheels can wobble and come off. The reason for these kinds of failures is that we learn significant leadership lessons at every incremental stage of growth and expanded level. If we leapfrog too many stages and levels or advance too quickly, we find ourselves missing key lessons in both leadership development and character formation.

In each of these four assignments, the developmental force was so potent in forging command confidence, because learning meant not simply job advancement, but more often survival. According to McCall "Learning was something you did because you didn't have much choice – you had to take action even if they were unsure of what you were doing."[62]

How do you get it? Be experiencing *Weight + Wins*. Where Do You Get It? During high school you get it on the job, on a team, and in a club. During college you get it as a volunteer leader, or on the job supervising others. In the post-college years you get it on the job, supervising and leading others.

A Major By-Product of Command Confidence: An *Expanding Sphere* of Influence

Command confidence forms when the weight of responsibility presses in on you plus a win, a positive outcome from leading others. When you add **time** to the *'weight plus the win'* equation, you often get a new by-product: an expanded sphere of influence.

Weight of Responsibility + Wins + Time = Expanding Sphere of Influence

As multiple layers of command confidence form and stack together over time, they also widen to extend your sphere of influence. When you gain a measure of proficiency at one level of responsibility, what often follows is a new assignment with greater responsibility. With the many stages and levels of leadership you move through as you grow command confidence, what is key is that at each level you learn essential new lessons needed to lead well. Whether or not you learn those new lessons may influence your upward trajectory. This is where many people hit a glass ceiling and their sphere of influence remains the same or even recedes. This is not to say everyone increases their sphere of influence if they are good. This equation, *'Weight + Wins + Time = An Expanded Sphere of Influence,'* is more of a general principle than a rigid law. While many people who develop layers of command confidence experience this, how much that sphere of influence actually expands is more often a blend of Divine and human efforts.

I experienced this expanding sphere of influence as a student leader in my college ministry. After transferring to Cal Poly San Luis Obispo from community college, I began attending the college group at Grace Church. With over three hundred students active, they did a great job reaching out to the new students. In the spring of my first year, I was invited to attend the college group leadership retreat. Largely a recruiting event for the next year's leaders, I was asked to head up the visitation ministry, responsible for visiting new students and helping them plug into the college group as a whole. That next year, our visitation team experienced a 'win' and enjoyed seeing many new students join the college group. After that year heading the visitation team, I was asked to become a divisional leader overseeing the new leader of the visitation team and two other ministry team leaders. With that year going well, -- experiencing another 'win', I was asked to head up the entire college group leadership team the following year.

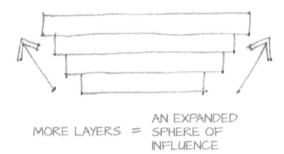

MORE LAYERS = AN EXPANDED SPHERE OF INFLUENCE

The combined weight of responsibility pressing in on me at each level of ministry, and by God's grace, experiencing many little 'wins', plus the natural time increment of a school year, equaled an expanding sphere of influence. Again, this equation is more of a general principle than a law of leadership. For some, the move up to an expanded sphere of influence brings lessons that direct you to step back down a level in order to be the most fruitful. A number of years ago, my good friend Jim Carlson was promoted to oversee the arts programs for all California prisons. He had worked for many years heading up the arts program at Folsom prison (made famous by Johnny Cash). Jim experienced many 'wins' at Folsom, masterfully impacting hundreds of inmates over the years. Naturally, when the position at the state level opened up, Jim was the best candidate and appointed director of all arts programs. After a couple years in executive leadership, it became evident to him that he was better suited to lead the arts program at Folsom than the entire state program. He missed working with the inmates and local staff so he put in for a transfer back down to Folsom. With a broadened perspective that came from state level experiences, Jim returned to his old job and experienced a new season of vitality and influence. Bigger is not always better. This expanding sphere of influence has some predictable stages in an institutional or corporate setting as well as in a church or volunteer run organization. It begins with self-leadership, where an individual is recognized as reliable, knowledgeable, personable, and shows initiative. Those qualities lead to becoming a 'Go-To' person who is sought after for counsel or expertise. This kind of expanded sphere of influence can flow all the way up to institutional leadership. You can see this pattern in the following diagram and charts.

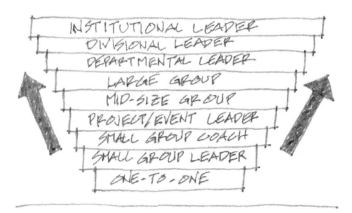

INSTITUTIONAL LEADER
DIVISIONAL LEADER
DEPARTMENTAL LEADER
LARGE GROUP
MID-SIZE GROUP
PROJECT/EVENT LEADER
SMALL GROUP COACH
SMALL GROUP LEADER
ONE-TO-ONE

AN EXPANDING
SPHERE OF
INFLUENCE

Spheres of Influence in an Institutional/Corporate Setting
(approximate descending order)

Board Leadership
(Multiple stakeholders & peers)
Institutional Leadership
(Multiple leaders & their teams, overall vision, mission & finances)
Divisional Leadership
(Multiple departmental leaders & their teams)
Departmental Leadership
(Multiple leaders & their teams)
Large Group
(Team with sub-leaders, 40+ people)
Mid-Size Group
(Team, <40 people)
Project/Event Leadership
(High-task orientation team)
Small Group
(Discussion group, research group, < 15)
One-on-One
('Go-To' person sought after for counsel or expertise)
Self-Leadership
(Reliable, knowledgeable, personable, initiative)

Spheres of Influence in a Church Setting
(approximate descending order)

Institutional Leadership: Senior pastor/Lead pastor
Divisional Leadership: Associate pastor/director
Departmental Leadership: Coordinate multiple volunteer leaders or teachers
Large Group 40+: Coordinate multiple leaders in one large class or group
Mid-Size Group <40: Sunday School or adult education teacher or coordinator
Project/Event Leadership: Men's, women's, youth, or children special events leader
Coach of Small Group Leaders: Typically 4 to 6 leaders
Small Group <15: Small Group Bible study leader
One-on-One: 'Go-To' person sought after for counsel or expertise
Self-Leadership: Reliable, knowledgeable, personable, initiative

---

There are exceptions related to how one's sphere of influence expands. Those with highly entrepreneurial wiring can leap-frog to the top of an organization. This is where they have the command confidence and risk-capacity to start the new company or new venture.

These expanding spheres of influence have predictable stages in business, corporate, and church settings. The layers of command confidence are forged while leading others and the weight of responsibility is on your back. These layers don't come from only leading, but leading *well*, having a "win", receiving legitimate positive feedback on your leadership performance. It is the "weight" plus the "win" that creates a game-changing combination.

To Conclude

In *Hoosiers*, one of the classic basketball movies of all time, Norman Dale arrives in the rural Indiana town of Hickory as a new high school teacher and the basketball coach. He had lost a previous prestigious coaching position after punching a student, so he is under pressure to succeed and dig himself out of a hole. Due to a small school enrollment, Dale has only a few players on his team. But, when his strict rules are disobeyed, he dismisses a key member from the team. The coach alienates the small town residents because he is not producing results fast enough and he is continually losing his temper. He gets himself ejected from more than one game. Dale is feeling the "weight" of responsibility but definitely not the "win."

By the middle of the season it is not looking good and an emergency town meeting is called to vote on whether Dale should be dismissed. In the heat of the debate, Jimmy Chitwood, the star player who quit the team earlier in the season sides with Dale. At the last minute, as the town votes him out, Chitwood asks permission to speak: he says he's ready to begin playing basketball again, but only if Dale remains as coach. The vote is dropped and from this point on, Hickory becomes an unstoppable team.

The team advances through tournament play, with contributions from Chitwood and a handful of unsung players. Hickory shocks the state by reaching the state championship game. In a large arena and before a crowd bigger than any they've seen, the Hickory players face long odds to defeat a team from South Bend, whose players are bigger, taller and faster. But with Chitwood scoring at the last second, tiny Hickory takes home the 1952 Indiana state championship and Norman Dale has forged fresh layers of command confidence, the "weight" of responsibility plus the "win."[63]

Personal Reflection...

1. What are some of your earliest memories of leading something?

2. In those early times, did you experience the "Weight + Win"? What did that feel like?

3. Can you recall a season where you feel like you developed layers of command confidence? What did that look like?

4. List the kinds of things you've led or been responsible for over the years. Can you see an expanding sphere of influence pattern?

5. Can you think of a time where you experienced a major challenge in leading something? What lessons do you recall from that?

Igniting Future
When you think about others you're investing in...

1. Can you identify how have they gained command confidence in the past?

2. What can you do to increase the likelihood of "weight + wins" for them? i.e. scaffolding experiences or giving them tracks to run on that have genuine responsibility and a high likelihood they will do well.

3. Are there any roadblocks that might hinder their developing command confidence?

4. What might be some "pre-leadership" qualities/habits/attitudes you could encourage them to develop?

5. What could you do to help them see expanding spheres of influence or the potential of them down the road?

Chapter 4

TURBO CONFIDENCE

The Reward of Intense Life Lessons

She was born 20th of 22 children and born prematurely. Because of racial segregation she was not allowed to be cared for at the local hospital. Her parents were hardworking and very poor. She was a very sickly child. Her mother nursed her through each illness until she had to go to the doctor when it was discovered that her left leg and foot were weak and becoming deformed. She had polio and there was no cure. Her parents took her to a medical college in Nashville...she learned to walk with a metal leg brace and all her brothers and sisters encouraged her to be strong and work very hard to rehabilitate. By her early teens she was able to walk normally and decided that she wanted to learn to run. Excelling first at basketball, she was a star who led her team to a state championship. Confident in her athleticism, and assisted by the same work ethic she developed while rehabilitating herself after the polio – she went on to become a track star, she is one of the most celebrated female athletes of all time...becoming the first

American woman to win three gold medals in an Olympics. Her name? *Wilma Rudolph!* In the midst of those challenging situations Wilma developed *Turbo Confidence.*

What Is Turbo Confidence?

I don't know about you, but I have never met anyone who has intentionally thrown himself under the bus just to build character. This layer of confidence is forged over a short and often intense period of time when life itself presses in on you to shape your character. It could be a major illness you or a loved one experiences; a career setback: job turmoil, demoted, fired; financial hardships; or a major friend loss (a fight or other issue that separates). It is a layer of confidence that is forged when we experience God's power to sustain us and carry us through dark difficult times. It is a vivid result of the truth "I will never leave you nor forsake you." The Lord has shown himself faithful and took care of me in my last time of turmoil so he can be trusted to do the same in the future. When "God is for me, *who* can be against me?"

This is not the miraculous healing from cancer, or the 11th hour rescue from trouble. It is the promise of God's presence, his sustaining power beyond our human capacity to endure that molds this layer of confidence. We could also call this *"divine confidence"* in lieu of *"turbo confidence"* because the source of the confidence is God alone. Look at what James writes about this in James 1:2-4: "Dear brothers and sisters, when troubles of any kind come your way, consider it an opportunity for great joy. ³ For you know that when your faith is tested, your endurance has a chance to grow. ⁴ So let it grow, for when your endurance is fully developed, you will be perfect and complete, needing nothing."

Bitter or Better?

It is a no-brainer that all of us go through intense hardships one time or another, but what is unique among the leaders I interviewed is that they all tended to come through these hardships transformed, better than before, more seasoned, and more fruitful. Rather than seeing the difficult times as detrimental or emotionally scarring, these people saw them (granted, after the fact, in the rearview mirror) as formative and highly influential. "Thinking of yourself as someone who is able to overcome tremendous adversity often leads to behavior that confirms that self-conception..."[64]

How Do You Get It?

Turbo confidence is formed through these trial-by-fire experiences as you call out to God for help. He comforts and sustains you, and you make it through. This process is like the painful development of callouses that build up on the fingertips through the hours, weeks, and months of guitar practice. Turbo confidence comes, not from being removed from difficult experiences, but by the sustaining grace of God as you endure them. It is the memory of your endurance that makes you stronger for future challenges yet to come.

An Ancient Example:

Recognizing their need for perspective about the trials they were facing, the Apostle Paul wrote to the church in Corinth in 2 Corinthians 1:8-10: "We do not want you to be uninformed, brothers, about the hardships we suffered in the province of Asia. We were under great pressure, far beyond our ability to endure, so that we despaired even of life. ⁹Indeed, in our hearts we felt the sentence of death. <u>But this happened that we might not rely on ourselves but on God</u>, who raises the dead. [10] He has delivered us from such a deadly peril, and he will deliver us. On him we have set our hope that he will continue to deliver us, [11]as you help us by your prayers."

Turbo confidence here is rooted in God Himself. What was the purpose of these hardships? To build their reliance on God. To believe that God would come through for them. Notice how verse 10 reveals a kind of turbo confidence. It says "He will continue to deliver us." This forges our turbo confidence in our belief that He came through for us here and He'll do it again. Look also at the role of prayer in building turbo confidence. Paul says "as you help us *by your prayers*." Paul was counting on God's deliverance being ignited by the prayers of others.

There are four distinct phases in the formation of turbo confidence.

1. Trial by Fire
2. Cry out to God for help
3. Help comes from God
4. You make it through with stronger faith

In the first phase, *Trial by Fire*, you face a major life challenge, far beyond your ability to control. Second, *You Cry Out To God For Help*, pleading with him to intervene. The writer of Hebrews reiterates this in Hebrews 4:16, "Let us then approach God's throne of grace with confidence, so that we may receive mercy and find grace to help us in our time of need." In the third phase, *Help Comes from God*, you receive his mercy and grace. You experience his presence, peace, and hope. The Psalmist echoes this in Psalm 121, "I lift up my eyes to the hills— where does my help come from? [2] My help comes from the LORD, the Maker of heaven and earth." In the fourth phase, *You Make It Through*, you see light at the end of the tunnel. You feel the warmth of the sun on your face again; you begin to breathe fresh Narnian-like air. While you may not be conscious of it at the time, you have forged a new layer of turbo confidence. Our self-awareness of this turbo confidence comes into play when we face another *Trial By Fire* and we look back at how the Lord brought us through the last time. He can be counted on to bring us through again.

You see a similar pattern displayed in what Paul writes in Romans 5:2-5, "And we rejoice in the hope of the glory of God. [3]Not only so, but we also rejoice in our sufferings" Why in the world would we be happy for suffering? "Because we know that suffering produces perseverance; [4]perseverance, character; and character, hope. [5]And hope does not disappoint us, because God has poured out his love into our hearts by the Holy Spirit, whom he has given us."

[Suffering → Perseverance → Character → Hope] = Turbo Confidence

Suffering builds our perseverance as we hang in there in the midst of hardship and we develop the greater capacity to endure. With perseverance our character deepens and we gain a reputation for being one who consistently holds on tight. With character formation comes hope—a future optimism. A key ingredient in the mix here is "God's love poured into our hearts" (v.5). He has not abandoned us in our suffering. His presence and his love comfort and sustain us to give us hope to endure in the fires of life. You can also gain perseverance and hope from hearing the stories of God working in the lives of others. Notice Romans 15:4, "For everything that was written in the past was written to teach us, so that through endurance and the encouragement of the Scriptures we might have hope."

When Do You Get It?

The High School and College Years?
During the high school years, faith-stretching or faith-crisis experiences and personal tragedies and hardships are the most common ways in which Turbo Confidence is built. But most of these events are not chosen; they are unexpected occurrences in life. During the college years, 33% of those I interviewed had turbo confidence building experiences. The most common types are the faith-stretching/faith-crisis experiences variety related to choices. Pastor Michael Foss recalled the faith-crisis in his college years of

becoming a Buddhist and then turning back to his Christian faith. "I had some Christian friends that were part of the university and that was a great group and we just did a lot of fun things together as well as we met and prayed and had Bible study. I dropped out of that group, in part because I left the Christian faith, and fancied myself a Buddhist for two years. It was a remarkable experience of grace to be brought back into faith and I ended up going back to my church at the end of my second year of college."[65]

Another California pastor, told me about a faith-crisis that started with his membership in the radical Black Panthers:

> During college, I was in the Black Panther Party, and I was full of anger. This was during the '60's when the radical movement and rebellion was a cool thing and a young white guy came to witness to me. He came and sat at our table, --the Black Panther Table we had just set up. At the time, everybody, Whites, Blacks, and Hispanics, would sit at their own tables, but he came and sat at our table. That's when my whole life started turning around because I stood up to fight him. I started picking on him, talking about his mother and stuff just to try to get him to swing at me. I was boxing at that time too, and I was teaching the people in the Black Panther Party how to shoot, how to hurt people, so I wanted him to swing at me that way I could have an excuse to not get kicked out of college. He had a briefcase that said "Rejoice in Jesus, the Messiah." I started hollering at him, "Are you one of those religious fanatics, one of those Holy Rollers?" And he jumped up and screamed at me and said "if you mean if I love God, I sure do." He did it twice and then I had an encounter with God because when I jumped up and tried to hit him, in front

of all those people in the cafeteria, I froze right there, I mean, I had an encounter. I couldn't move my arm. I could not do anything and I'm standing up there trying to hit this guy and couldn't hit him. I don't know how long I was frozen in this position, but when I could move again everybody began to laugh. Nobody would have ever laughed at me before.

I didn't know what to do because I really was a Black Panther, but I think I turned into a Pink Panther after that! I took off and I ran but that guy ran after me until I stopped. Then he started talking about how God loves me and I didn't want to know anything about God because I don't believe in God. God is a white man's religion and all that stuff.

For three months that guy never left me alone. Every time he'd see me he'd throw his hands up and say "Praise the Lord" and other stuff. He just worked me over and when by the third month I couldn't shake him. He had a little booklet and said "if you let me share this with you I'll leave you alone." I was ready for him to leave me alone. I was starting to see through that little book and after going through many trials and tribulations I opened my heart and asked Christ to come in.[66]

Northern California Pastor Larry Adams, lost his step-dad and he quit school to take care of his mom and younger brothers:

In my third year of college my step-dad, who raised me, died suddenly. I felt at the time as the oldest son and with the two brothers in high school, and my mom in that situation, I immediately felt a weight of responsibility. So, rightly or wrongly, I decided that I was going to take a break from school, after three years and

92

I was going to work in case there was a need to provide. No one asked me to do it, I just assumed it.[67]

All these experiences were formative in building turbo confidence.

Bob, a senior pastor of more than one megachurch, experienced a major faith-crisis in high school. His dad was a pastor who he deeply respected. Bob recalled:

> One of the things that was very big in my life is that I'm a doubter and I remember one time, I would go to my dad's library and pull out books on assurance of salvation. I would read whatever I could. My folks didn't know because I didn't have the courage to tell them, that I really doubted. I was sincere, I prayed, I accepted the Lord when I was six years old. I remember one time when I couldn't stand it any longer so I went in and I said to my mother, "I don't know if I'm saved?" Well that must have been a shock to them and they gave me all the answers they had. We talked about it I don't know how many times and that was a big struggle to me."

He made it through his faith-crisis and formed turbo confidence.

When and How Do You Get It During The Post-College Years And Beyond?

In the post-college, career years, Turbo Confidence is a byproduct of personal tragedies and on-the-job. The four most common types of turbo confidence building experiences in this season are:[68]

1. **"Personal tragedies** teach sensitivity to others, how to cope when things are beyond your control, and how to recognize your own personal limitations."[69] It's one thing when you

lose your great grandfather, it's another when a classmate succumbs to leukemia.

2. **"Career setbacks**, such as missed promotions, demotions, or being fired teach us hard lessons on organizational politics, coping strategies, and about our personal limits.

3. **Business failures** often bring deep lessons in humility, handling relationships, and coping with events beyond your control.

4. **Subordinate performance problems** allow you to learn both empathy and how to confront when needed."[70]

Sometimes Turbo Confidence can be self-induced if we get ourselves into trouble, but eventually learn from our mistakes. *Executive Derailment* is a fairly recent term used to describe what happens to employees who rise through the ranks of organizations or institutions with strong track records of success and then get sidetracked...they either get fired, demoted, or passed over for promotion. In their book *Developing Global Executives*, authors McCall and Hollenbeck note six key errors leading to derailment:

1. Failing to listen to advice and feedback
2. Refusing to change when change was needed
3. Behaving in ways that alienate other people
4. Bungling relationships with key people
5. Failure to take needed actions or to deliver on promises, and failure to ask for help
6. Selecting ineffective people to fill positions[71]

Also, in the following chart, notice the diverse early childhood and family backgrounds of the forty senior pastors in the original study. Seventy-five percent considered their early home life a nurturing environment, 25% non-nurturing. And 40% experienced a family crisis such as the death or major illness of a parent or sibling.

Early Childhood and Family Background (N=40)[72]

Variables	Percent
Birth order:	
First born	60%
Middle	20%
Last born	20%
Raised by:	
Mom & dad:	85%
Mom or dad:	15%
Grandparents:	5%
Parent's occupations:	
Father: Senior Pastor	13%
Professional	35%
Service sector	45%
Mother: Homemaker	68%
Professional	8%
Service sector	20%
Home environment:	
Nurturing	75%
Non-nurturing	25%
Experienced family crisis	40%
Parent(s)' church	
Active in same church	70%
Inactive in any church	20%
Active in other church	10%
Socioeconomic status	
lower income	18%
lower to middle income	33%
middle income	38%
upper middle income	13%

To Conclude

Turbo confidence is a layer of confidence that you can't intentionally forge yourself. No one in their right mind throws themselves under the bus to build character. However, you can prepare for it by deepening your faith and trust in God himself. In the middle of crises you learn of his majesty and sovereign power alongside of his grace, mercy, and compassion. You also learn that he is a God you can count on. In Hebrews 13:5 it says "he will never leave you or forsake you,"[73] and in Hebrews 4:16 it says that you can "approach the throne of grace with confidence". When the time comes and you find yourself in the midst of the fire you can turn to him with confidence.

This layer of confidence is forged over a short and intense period of time when life itself acts to shape your character. The Apostle Peter sums up Turbo Confidence up well in I Peter 5:10-11, "And the God of all grace, who called you to his eternal glory in Christ, after you have suffered a little while, will himself restore you and make you strong, firm and steadfast. [11] To him be the power for ever and ever. Amen."

Now that we have identified the primary levels of confidence, we can turn to the epoxy-like seams that hold these experiences together and help bear the weight of life in the lives of high impact people. That's what we'll do in the next four chapters.

Personal Reflection...

1. Can you think of someone you know who has developed Turbo Confidence after enduring a major difficulty? Describe their experience.

2. Can you recall a time someone close to you went through a challenge or crisis, but did not develop turbo confidence afterwards? What might have hindered them?

3. Can you think of a time when you faced a colossal challenge or hardship where the Lord didn't remove you, but sustained you? Maybe you did not "consider it all joy" at the time, but can see in retrospect how God was truly working.

4. When you face adversity, what could you do differently in light of what you've learned about Turbo Confidence? What might change your response in the future?

Igniting Future
When you think about others you're investing in...

1. While you're not going to throw anyone under the bus to gain this, what could you do in hindsight, after someone has experienced significant adversity to be able to learn from it?

2. How might you be able to help prepare others to grow layers of Turbo Confidence in the face of difficulty?

3. What do you feel are some things to avoid when talking with someone in the midst of a crisis?

4. What could be said or done to others in the midst of a crisis or major challenge that would have a positive impact?

Chapter 5

CONVICTIONS

Key Ingredients for Change

Growing up with two brothers and a sister much older than I, I rarely had hand-me-downs or old toys passed down to me. Occasionally I would claim or co-opt a neglected baseball glove, football helmet, or board game. One summer between third and fourth grade, I put on my own garage sale. To make some spare change for the neighborhood ice cream truck, I sold some of my less-than-perfect toys and games, plus many of my brother's and sister's stuff I deemed "currently unused". When my sister, came outside to see how the sale was going, she was aghast to see her two Barbie dolls for sale. I reminded her she hadn't played with them for years, but it was the emotional connection she had with them that fueled her concerns. She eventually relented and I sold them for the equivalent of two ice cream bars. Years later, watching the evening news, she saw that original, first-run Barbies were now collector's items and selling for a chunk of change. She was quick to remind me her two dolls were originals and worth a fortune.

It wasn't until my early thirties that I recall having something of great value passed down to me. My mom gave me my dad's wristwatch after he died. Part of what made that watch so special is that when I was in junior high I remember going to the jewelry store with my mom when she bought it for my dad's birthday. It was a classic, brushed silver Seiko and my dad loved it. It sat in a box in my dresser drawer for years until recently I took it in and had it cleaned up. Every time I put that watch on I fondly think of my dad.

Something else of my dad's that was not officially passed along to me, but was far more valuable than a wristwatch, was his strong work ethic. Growing up in a family of nine kids during the depression, he learned how to work hard. He had a conviction about getting up early and putting in a good day's work. He used to say "When you wake up, get up, don't sleep your life away!" I've rarely ever been able to sleep in past 7:00 and usually get up and get going before 6:00. His conviction became my own.

Convictions are the first of four epoxy-like seams (ELS). There are four specific ELS's that influence the forming of the four layers of confidence. They are so pivotal to this whole process that an entire chapter is devoted to each one.

"This will be on the test," is a phrase practically guaranteed to awaken the most passive, preoccupied, and disengaged students. I would like to say the same thing about this chapter. *Instilling Convictions* is disproportionately influential among the chapters of this book. If you were to remove it, and yet vigorously apply the principles from the other chapters, you could without a doubt inspire scores of people with capacity to change the world. What would be in question is changing the world into what? That depends on what your convictions are.

What Are Convictions?

Convictions are much stronger than beliefs. They are like beliefs on steroids. Convictions are extremely strong beliefs or presumptions that drive your behavior, your choices, and fuel your dreams. Beliefs are truths, concepts, or ideas we trust or place our confidence in, but they don't always influence behavior.

The main difference between convictions and beliefs is the degree to which they actually govern your behavior.Many of us "believe" things to be true, but those beliefs don't always change the way we live. Many people believe that they should save enough money for a rainy day, but most don't (64% according to one national survey)[74]. Many people "believe" God rewards good and punishes evil, but they still do evil. Many "believe" in God, but are not ready to make lifestyle choices in light of that belief. What we believe and how strongly we hold to those beliefs, combine to form our convictions. The decisions we make and the actions we take reveal our convictions.

Convictions, by their very nature, provide us with an intense blend of motivational fuel and moral guard rails. Convictions compel. They provide the thrust we need to start new healthy habits or to stop bad ones. They give us moral navigation and help us avoid danger zones.

Convictions provide motivational fuel for life

Convictions become like motivational rocket fuel for breaking free of earth's gravitational forces. Having the conviction that a college education is critical to your future career produces the motivational fuel to endure boring lectures, academic red tape, financial hardships, and the most annoying of room-mates. Having the conviction that Christian schools or parochial schools are what your kids need can give you the boost to get a second job. The conviction that a good friend is worth more than gold can give us staying power to overlook offenses and hurt feelings. The conviction to make disciples of all nations can send field workers to the farthest corners of the earth. The conviction to honor and care for an aging parent can bring field workers home from international assignments. The conviction to love your neighbor as yourself can motivate you to sacrificial acts way outside your comfort zone. Jack Graham, pastor of Prestonwood Baptist Church in the Dallas area, says his conviction that outreach is of the utmost importance came early in life. "I have always wanted to do whatever it takes to fulfill the great commission, to reach people." To "Go and make disciples of all nations..." was a conviction that was formed growing up in church and influenced his entire career.[75]

Convictions are like battering rams and produce the force of character to push through obstacles and roadblocks of life. Particularly, our convictions about the character of God can give us the resolve to persevere in the face of the most intense challenges. Isaiah was an uncompromising, sincere, and compassionate prophet and poet. In Isaiah 50:7, we see a compelling picture of one of the strongest convictions to do what God desires. He writes, "Because the Sovereign LORD helps me, I will not be dismayed. Therefore, I have set my face like a stone, determined to do his will."[76] Isaiah had the conviction that God was on his side and He would actually help him out, --that God is the sovereign ruler of the universe and more than able to help him.

Convictions become our moral compass

Convictions also act as moral guard rails to keep us on the right path. The Psalmist could confidently pray in Psalm 119:32 "I run in the path of your commands, for you have set my heart free." Similarly in Psalm 119:101 he writes "I have kept my feet from every evil path so that I might obey your word." Our convictions help us navigate difficult life terrain, marking out the paths we are to follow and the detours we should avoid. Here are some examples: the conviction to date only those who share your faith places firm boundary markers for potential spouses; the conviction to give generously to your church first above other causes and needs; the conviction to not cheat on your taxes because you believe it's wrong to lie and shade the truth; the conviction to err on the side of compassion when faced with requests for spare change from those less fortunate; and the conviction to not spend time outside of work with the attractive co-worker when you're already married.

Convictions don't tell you a destination, they function more like wayfinding. "Wayfinding is the ancient art of figuring out where you are going when you don't actually know your destination. For wayfinding, you need a compass and you need a direction not a map – a direction."[77] Convictions can give you a truth north.

A Tale of Two Bridges

I grew up on the northern edge of the California coastal town of Santa Barbara. At the end of my street there was a deep, jungle-like ravine with a creek running through that emptied into the Pacific Ocean two miles away. Every day I rode my bike across a white wooden footbridge over that ravine on my way to Kellogg Elementary. Down in the ravine, after school, my friends and I caught tadpoles and frogs, fought imaginary battles, and built bamboo rafts with dreams to sail to the Channel Islands. Though our ravine didn't come equipped with the same safety features of a McDonald's Playland, we knew about stranger-danger and we knew our boundaries. We ran all through that ravine; across moss-covered rocks, over fallen trees, and up sandy slopes, but we always knew our limits, how far we could go. As long as we could still see the white footbridge we were good. If we went to where we could see the railroad trestle crossing the ravine, we had gone too far and were supposed to turn back. The railroad trestle was more than an arbitrary boundary. It was a danger zone. Train-hopping drifters camped under that trestle all year round and were not known to be friendly to adventurous kids invading their territory. Those two bridges were like our convictions, like moral guardrails that keep us out of trouble and on the right path.

How Do We Develop Convictions?

What causes some beliefs to rise to the level of convictions, or increase in temperature from cold to hot? Is it after hearing a stirring sermon, drying our eyes after an emotionally charged movie, or simply being told by mom or dad what to believe? Convictions are rarely forged after one exposure, regardless of intensity. An idea or belief, moving into the realm of a conviction comes more by absorbing them from the groups and communities we belong to. As we almost unconsciously absorb them, over time we eventually fully embrace them. Absorbing and embracing take place in communities like our family and extended family, at church, in school, on the job, on a team, or in a club. One rule of absorption: you can only absorb something you are in close contact with.

Sometimes absorbing is a good thing. We only want paper towels that are the best at soaking up our messes, or diapers that are the finest at absorption and don't leak. Other times being good at absorbing is not the best. When we spill our drink on the novel we just borrowed from a friend, or on the front seat of our new car, or when we pull our favorite sweatshirt out

106

of the drawer at the last minute and it still smells like the campfire smoke it absorbed last summer.

There are four factors to absorbing and embracing convictions that take place within the context of community:

1. ***Strong Sense of Belonging to a Community***
2. ***Attractive Modeling by People of Influence in the Community***
3. ***Active Engagement in the Mission and Work of the Community***
4. ***Personal Reflection upon Community Convictions***

1. A Strong Sense of Belonging to a Community

The first step to absorbing new convictions is to feel like you are part of that community, --you belong, whether it's church, school, or even your own family. When we feel like an outsider to a new group our defenses are up, our identity is independent, and we see ourselves as a separate entity. When we feel a strong sense of belonging, we naturally identify the beliefs and values of the community as our own. The absorption now has a chance to begin. Beginning to belong is like taking the plastic wrap off of a new sponge. It could even be the most absorbent sponge money can buy, but if it's still sealed in plastic it won't absorb.

Emile Durkheim, considered the father of social science, along with well-known developmental psychologist, Jean Piaget, believed "morality resulted from social interaction or immersion in a group. However, Durkheim believed moral development was a natural result of attachment to the group, an attachment which manifests itself in a respect for symbols, rules, and authority of that group."[78]

Many years ago I had the privilege of teaching second and third grade Sunday school at my church. My incentive was that my youngest son, Hudson, was in that class. Having been a pastor for many years, teaching in the children's ministry has been the domain of others much more gifted for that context than I. But that year, I led a small group of boys and watched many of them move from the fringes of newcomer, to really belonging. Sam first began coming to class with his older cousin. He was shy and a bit reserved. Week after week he kept coming, sometimes with his cousin, sometimes on his own. Eventually, he started to speak up during our small groups and play with other kids in class. One day after church I was talking with his dad and he said that Sam raves about his Sunday school class. He can't wait to get there. He was beginning to feel like he belonged.

I have to confess that even though I grew up in Southern California, I was never a big USC fan. However, my first day of class as a doctoral student at USC turned out to be surprisingly influential in changing my allegiance. Sporting a USC logo Hawaiian shirt, my professor, Dr. Stu Gothold, stepped to the podium and welcomed all of us, not just to the class, but into the Trojan Family. A former Superintendent of the Los Angeles Unified School District and a devoted USC alum, Dr. Gothold began to passionately expound on the benefits of being part of this devoted family. A funny thing happened, it wasn't instantaneous, but I began to pay more attention to the SC football team scores, watch more games, and talk about those games with anyone who would listen. I started to feel like I belonged to the Trojan family.

2. Attractive Modeling by People of Influence in the Community

Much like vicarious confidence, we absorb convictions from people we look up to and those we admire. They begin to form as you watch those you respect live them out. David Brooks, the New York Times columnist and author of *The Social Mind*, believes that we develop convictions or character through a "learning-to-see model" and that "character emerges gradually out of the mysterious interplay of a million little good influences."[79] There is no question that moms and dads play a massive role in developing convictions.[80] Grandparents are also especially influential on kids in single parent homes.[81] We also absorb convictions from older brothers and sisters, teachers, professors, pastors, Sunday school teachers, coaches, and bosses we respect. According to Stanford psychologist Bill Damon, people must believe that "I personally can make a difference." This conviction, this intention to take action, he says, is why it's so important to have observed a role model enact purpose in their own life. "You have to believe that your efforts will not be in vain."[82]

A Parent's Benchmark
Bob Russell recalled how he learned from his mom and dad that you never miss church. He said:

> I have a memory of waking up one Sunday morning, and I guess about 18 inches of snow had fallen the night before, and I thought that this was one Sunday we wouldn't have to go to church, since we were going about 15 miles away. My Dad piled us all in the car, and started plowing, and going to church, and we got about a half mile away from home and got stuck. So we trudge back home, and my brother and I thought, well we'll get to play

games today. Not so. They sat us down in the living room and my Dad took out the Bible and read the Bible, and my sister plunked out some choruses on the piano while we all tried to sing. My Mother went into the kitchen and got some saltine crackers and some grape Kool-aide, and we had communion in our living room. I tell people, you know, that is probably the most memorable church service I have ever attended. But, that discipline (that conviction) that you never miss church, for a little bit of snow, or a little bit of sickness, you just keep going. That was instilled in me early, and that really left a lifelong impression on me.[83]

A Family's Influence

The Apostle Paul's protégé Timothy, absorbed the basics of his genuine faith from his family. For many kids, the family's church and religion are thrust upon them and they develop almost a hard-shell coating preventing authentic faith from growing. But Paul tells us that for Timothy it was much different. Not only did his mom influence him, but his grandmother had an impact on the caliber of his faith, as well. In 2 Timothy 1:5 Paul says, "I have been reminded of your sincere faith, which first lived in your grandmother Lois and in your mother Eunice and, I am persuaded, now also lives in you."

A Church's Influence

In his early forties, Harley Allen left his career in sales to become the senior pastor of a small struggling church in northern California. He went on to see that church grow strong, with thousands attending by the time he retired. Harley recalled how influential his church was at building his convictions when he was young. He shared with me, "I was grounded early as a young man that God had a purpose for my life. In those early years of my church upbringing, our pastor was very good at saying you are put here for a reason. It isn't just all about you. I learned that at an early age."[84] Those were significant childhood lessons. He learned purpose and position as a child. And he learned them from his pastor, who was a model he respected and looked up to.

Joel Hunter, senior pastor of Northland Church in Orlando, learned key lessons in church as a young boy that later developed into life-long convictions. He shared, "I sensed when I went to church, somewhere along the line I got the idea that there was a God who loved me and who made me to contribute. I had this sense from as far back as I can remember that the reason that I was in the world was to make a positive impact, to make a difference."[85] That belief grew into a conviction that endured and influenced his impact on thousands over the years.

A Boss's Example

For two summers during college, I worked as a house painter. My boss, John Tillman, the son of Swedish immigrants, was active in my church and helped to lead memorable High Sierra backpack trips for our youth group. One day at work he mentioned all three of his daughters were going to be in college that year. I commented how expensive that was going to be for him. Without giving it any thought he said, "it's a good thing my father owns the cattle on a thousand hillsides." He didn't have to worry about the financial challenge. John really had the conviction that God had more than enough resources to meet his needs.

A Spouse's and Friends' Influence

Larry Osborne, one of the lead pastors at North Coast Church in Southern California, shared how his convictions about true spirituality were re-formed by the example of his wife and two good friends. "Two of my best buddies, and my wife, are all introverts. They had a major shift on my understanding of what spirituality is. I think leaders tend to think that spirituality is reflected in becoming a leader. People who have teaching gifts, usually have to read and study, but they love to learn and then share it. But these friends were very bright people, one had a PhD in photochemistry, and my wife is an accountant, but none of them liked to read, they wouldn't pick up the Bible and just be fascinated by what they read. They didn't talk to people about the Lord and their spirituality; but their spirituality was just like a deep river flowing inside. I think that altered my view of who I was trying to reach and what I was trying to make people into. I'm not trying to make everybody into a Silas or a Timothy, I mean Paul created an entourage and I hope, I think I have done a good job of doing that. But there are a lot of cobblers in Corinth. There are so many ways to show their love for Jesus, and that is the point. I'm not sure that in those early ministry days the leader in me valued that. Those years were a huge tilt for me, to come to understand that some of those people were a whole lot better than the "on fire" leaders who burned out, ran off with some woman. I did have three of my six early mentors really fall. That taught me that knowing how to teach the Bible or being aggressive in your conversations just might not be spirituality. Today, North Coast is the kind of church where we are not trying to make everybody into a leader. We just try to make you into you."[86]

3. Active Engagement in the Mission and Work of the Community

When we are actively engaged in the mission and work of the community it helps to personally solidify that community's convictions. Volunteering to be an usher at church, hosting a Bible study in your home, or working at the church food bank, all provide a level of engagement that helps to cement convictions. Giving time, energy, and effort to further the cause, whatever that may be, helps to move *beliefs* to become *convictions*. According to Dr. Timothy Wilson of the University of Virginia, change in our behavior comes before a change in our attitude, feelings, or convictions.[87] Aristotle has similarly said "We acquire virtues by first having put them into action"[88]

In the months that followed the devastating hurricane Katrina, I led a team of guys to Biloxi, Mississippi, to help rebuild homes for a week. Ryan, one of the guys on our team, had recently started attending our church. He worked in construction and added a ton of practical expertise to our team effort. He was also young in the faith but enthusiastically jumped in, taking a week off of work at his own expense. After we returned home Ryan's faith continued to grow and he started to lead a young adult's Bible study group. Later he went on to lead an entire singles ministry team at a larger church. Eventually he went back to college and got a degree in ministry and became a pastor. But it was during that week in Biloxi, serving on our team to rebuild homes of families he'd never met, that his conviction to serve others started to take lasting shape.

It was an influential high school missions trip to a Navajo Indian reservation in Arizona that my wife, Kirsten, recalled as an early convictions-building experience. Their main focus was to do a 'Vacation Bible School' for the elementary age kids. Kirsten experienced leading a small group of girls as they played games, had Bible lessons, and just got to know the kids on a deeper level. One of those girls, Yolanda, made a new commitment to the faith at the end of the week. This was one of the first times in Kirsten's life that seeds were planted and she began to learn the conviction of selflessness and serving others; putting their needs ahead of her own.

4. Personal Reflection Upon Community Convictions

Full absorption of beliefs into convictions comes with this fourth stage. Reflective engagement begins to happen during the high school years and beyond. This is where we consciously *embrace* certain convictions as we read devotional literature, or biographies of those revered in the community. We also draw them from the Bible, other books, songs, and authors we respect, "C.S. Lewis says..." or "Jane Austen says..." This also happens when our convictions are challenged and we have to dig deeper to make certain they are worth holding onto.

My first college philosophy class had that effect on me. During one lecture, my professor challenged the historical reliability of the Bible. Being relatively new to the faith at the time, I was dumbfounded that someone at that level of education could not trust the Bible. Challenged, I began to do my own research and found that my conviction to trust the historical reliability of the Bible skyrocketed. With my newly refined conviction, I engaged in class discussions with a greater confidence and passion.

One day on campus I ran into a high school friend I hadn't seen in a while, and found out he had been heavily involved in a religious cult. With similar zeal I discovered with my philosophy class, I began to learn more about the beliefs of my friend's cult. He and I would meet often to discuss and debate our own core beliefs about God, Jesus, the Holy Spirit, and the Church. I'd love to say my friend saw the light and left his cult behind but he didn't. What did happen was that my beliefs about God were deepened and forged into convictions in ways they had never been before.

To Conclude

Interestingly, from all the high impact leaders I interviewed, there were three particular convictions that rose to the top; a Christ-Centeredness, an others-first orientation, and living on-mission. To live with Christ at the center is at the heart of what Paul writes in Galatians 2:20, "I have been crucified with Christ and I no longer live, but Christ lives in me. The life I now live in the body, I live by faith in the Son of God, who loved me and gave himself for me." To live an others-first orientation is a life of service focused on the needs of others. You see this displayed in Mark 10:43-45, "Not so with you. Instead, whoever wants to become great among you must be your servant, and whoever wants to be first must be slave of all. For even the Son of Man did not come to be served, but to serve, and to give his life as a ransom for many." When this conviction develops it is almost like a conversion experience or a threshold where one part of your life you focused on yourself, your needs, desires, and wants, but then at some point you walked across the threshold of others-first and began to focus outward toward others. The third conviction, to live on-mission, is in some ways a combination of the first two. To live on-mission for God is to have a clear sense of purpose to your life and to live it with passion; to not just float along but to put a dent in the universe. I like Mark Twain's perspective on this. He said "The two most important days in your life are the day you were born and the day you find out why."[89]

Beliefs move from the territory of mental assent into the realm of conviction when we absorb them from the groups and communities we belong to and who infuse and model those beliefs in real life. Almost unconsciously we absorb them, and over time we eventually fully embrace them. One rule of absorption: you can only absorb something you are in close contact with.

115

Personal Reflection...

1. What do you think are your own most important convictions?

2. Where did you get your convictions? _Who_ or _what_ influenced you the most?

3. In what ways have you seen the four aspects (belonging, attractive modeling, active engagement, personal reflection) of conviction development played out in your life? Give an example of something that became a conviction for you?

4. How obvious is it that you are living out your convictions? Can your family, friends, and co-workers see them reflected in the way you live? What could you do to enhance that?

Igniting Future
When you think about others you're investing in...

1. As they have the potential to move on to new spheres of influence, what convictions would you want them to embrace?

2. What are you already doing to help them develop strong convictions? What could you do to expand that?

3. Who are their attractive models? Who else might be good models to expose them to?

4. Are they actively engaged in the mission & work of your community? If so, in what way? If not, what could they begin to do?

5. Is there anything you need to do differently to help them absorb and embrace those convictions?

Chapter 6

SELF-AWARENESS AND SPIRITUAL WHOLENESS

Correcting the Lenses of Self-Perception

*"My mother was a caterpillar and
my father was a worm,
but I'm OK with that"*
-Khalil,
Veggie Tales Jonah Movie

It was *Friar Tucks*, a quaint restaurant in the historic Sierra foothill town of Nevada City, that provided one of my first significant lessons in self-awareness. Kirsten and I were on one of our first dates. By that point I had a hunch my future-wife-to-be actually liked me. It felt almost euphoric, sitting across the table, our conversation effortlessly flowing from one topic to the next. It wasn't until three years after the wedding that she broke the news. "You talk too loud sometimes, honey," she said, fortunately with a smile and smirk. "Like when we were at *Friar Tucks* and everyone in the restaurant could hear what you had to say." Unbeknownst to me, while I was basking in the glow of our candlelit conversation, she was hoping I would lower my voice. Too embarrassed to say anything at the time, she waited until the right time to spring it on me. At first I tried to rationalize it that she just had sensitive hearing. It surely couldn't be that I actually talk too loud? But deep down I knew she was right. I was learning a lesson in self-awareness the hard way.

The shelves of almost any bookstore are loaded with books on leadership. If you scan their pages you are sure to find a chapter, a section, or at least a significant reference to the importance of self-awareness. Both ancient & contemporary thinkers highly recommend it. The ancients had another way to talk about self-awareness. They challenged us to "KNOW THYSELF." The phrase "Know Thyself" has been attributed to at least six ancient Greek sages, the most notable being Socrates.[90] The ancient Roman poet Juvenal states that the idea descended *de caelo* (from heaven).[91] King Solomon proclaimed the value of self-awareness when he wrote "The wisdom of the prudent is to give thought to their ways, but fools deceive themselves."[92] Personally, I love what Ann Landers says: "Know yourself. Don't accept your dog's admiration as conclusive evidence that you are wonderful."[93]

Based on his research on Emotional Intelligence, Daniel Goleman says that "self-awareness is the foundation of, and most essential of the emotional intelligence abilities."[94] It is invaluable for leaders in the corporate world. In one study of CEO's, it was found that the self-awareness was much greater for the CEO's of the best performing companies and the lowest for the worst performers.[95]

What Is Self-Awareness?

Think about it. Wherever you shop for sunglasses you will always find a mirror nearby. Retailers know it is not about how well your new shades enhance your vision, but how cool you look. To have self-awareness is to accurately see yourself as others see you. It is to be conscious of who you *are* and who you are *not*, to know intimately what you are good at and what you are not. It involves a heightened sense of your own personality, motivations, and moods. Self-Awareness is like a traffic signal to future progress. When you have it, green light! When you don't, red light! Or, at least slow down!

Three Components of Self-Awareness

In the article, *Self-Confidence and Leader Performance*, author D.T. Hall states that there are three key components that help us build the mirror of our own self-awareness:[96]

#1. IDENTITY Awareness

Identity awareness is knowing who you are, your dreams, desires, abilities, personality, and family background. In Romans 12:3, the Apostle Paul gives sound insight on Identity Awareness, "Don't think you are better than you really are. Be honest in your evaluation of yourselves, measuring yourselves by the faith God has given you." How would you describe yourself to others?

When I was a kid my dream was to become an architect. Now at the time I didn't realize how my family background would reinforce that. On my dad's side were inventors, engineers, and artisans. My great grandfather, John Cooper Tunnicliff, held many patents for innovative farming equipment. My grandfather was an accomplished land surveyor. On my mom's side they were farmers and preachers. My grandfather was a farmer and a John Deere dealer in the Texas Panhandle. My great grandfather A.J. was a Baptist preacher named after the famous missionary Adoniram Judson. Know your identity: What makes you, you. Funny, I did become an architect, but also a preacher!

#2. EMOTIONAL Awareness

A second component of self-awareness is emotional awareness. It's the ability to recognize your own inner state, your moods, motives, emotions. This is short-term like monitoring your blood pressure and heart-rate. "Wow, I'm kind of depressed today," or "I'm feeling edgy or cranky." Have you ever been surprised when someone told you that you were grouchy, irritable, or rude? You might just be surprised they noticed. But if their observation is news to you, it can be a major warning light that something under the hood needs attention.

#3. IMPACT Awareness:

A third component is impact awareness. This is where you recognize your impact on others. How you affect other people around you. This is about understanding how you are coming across to co-workers and friends. Getting along with others, and being able to read other's feelings, emotions, intentions, and desires. My professor, mentor, and friend, Dr. David Eckman, would tell our seminary classroom of future pastors that you need to know your persona. How you are actually coming across to others. Not to be self-absorbed, but to have a realistic view of how people perceive you. Impact awareness is like having relational radar, a kind of echolocation ability for interactions with others. An ability to know, *"Did I just totally offend her?" "Was I too insensitive or overbearing?"*

Tim (not his real name) was a guy in my church who had a strong conviction for the Bible. He could quote many verses off the tip of his tongue. At first he sounded deeply spiritual, but after a while you began to notice he was quoting the same five or six verses over and over again. He was also very abrasive and highly critical of anyone in authority. Though his conviction for the Bible was high, his self-awareness was in the cellar. Whenever people saw him coming they either went the other way or just never made eye contact. He had no clue what a difficult person he had become or that his impact awareness was in a death spiral.

Self-Awareness is essential for impacting others. Identity Awareness, Emotional Awareness, and Impact Awareness, these three combine to make up a well-rounded self-awareness.[97]

Four Levels of Clarity to Self-Awareness

How self-aware are you? In his groundbreaking book, *Emotional Intelligence: Why It Can Matter More Than IQ*, Daniel Goleman describes multiple levels of self-awareness, or degrees of clarity in how you see yourself. Based on my own experience, I have added one additional level to his list. On one end of the list is "crystal clear" clarity. On the other is "distorted" lacking an accurate sense of self awareness.[98]

1st. Crystal Clear *Highly Self-Aware*

This is when you are alert and responsive, aware of your moods as you are having them. You are in good emotional health, sure of your own boundaries, and tend to have a positive outlook on life. When you get into a bad mood, you don't ruminate and obsess about it, and are able to get out of it sooner than later. "I'm having a rotten morning!" Or as one Facebook friend put it "I'm wearing my grumpy pants today." Or another, "I'm having a great day!" or "Why am I so on edge today?"

Sand Harbor State Park in Lake Tahoe, Nevada, has the most amazing levels of clarity I have ever seen in a lake. Scrambling among the rock outcroppings along the shore you can see through the crystal clear water at the finest details of the sand and rock bottom twenty feet below. To have Sand Harbor-like clarity is to be able to see yourself accurately and have the internal strength to change bad moods and attitudes if necessary.

2nd. Patchy Fog *Accepting*

"This is when you are clear about what you are feeling, but you tend to be passively accepting of your moods, especially bad moods and so you don't try to change them. People who accept them with a laissez-faire attitude, do nothing to change them despite their distress. They are like depressed people who are resigned to their despair."[99] Charlie Brown's friend Lucy knew when she was crabby, but she wasn't about to change!

3rd. The Lights Are Off *Unaware*

This is one I added to Goleman's list of three. This is the person who is often humble, clueless, and without guile; "Wow, I never knew that about me?" This is like Jim Carrey in the Truman Show, totally unaware. He played a naive salesman who discovers that his entire life is secretly the focus of a popular TV show. Unaware people tend to be good natured, but reserved and other-centered in their outlook. This is the Absent-minded professor level of clarity.

4th. Distorted *Engulfed*

This is when you are overwhelmed and can't see straight. You feel totally swamped by your emotions and helpless to escape them. It's as though your brain has left the building and your own moods have taken over. They are in charge. You are emotionally out of control. As a result, you do little to try to escape bad moods, feeling that you have no control over your emotional life.[100]

How Do We Become More Self Aware?

How do we move towards the crystal clear level? How

can we increase our ability to have crystal clear identity awareness, emotional awareness, and impact awareness? In my research I found there were four shaping influences in the development of self-awareness: trial and error experiences, feedback and affirmation, significant learning experiences, and challenging life circumstances. Trial and error garnered the highest response at 39 percent of those interviewed. Feedback and affirmation were second at 24 percent, and critical events/challenging life circumstances were third at 12 percent.

#1. Through Trial and Error (39 percent)

Trial and error experiences were essentially learning what things you excel at and what you don't. This was a significant lesson in self-awareness. Clark Tanner, noted the trial and error process in farm work: "I think part of it came from my background growing up on a farm. We had to work hard and you just kind of did anything, you just had to try stuff. If it was going to get done, you had to do it. So I think a lot of it came by trial and error, and not necessarily believing in yourself so much, as it was, if it was going to get done, you had to do it."[101] I think sometimes you get this through a process of elimination. Sometimes you find out what you're not good at by just doing it and you say "Wow, I really lack an ability there." But then you find you have abilities in areas you may not have realized."[102]

Pastor Joel Hunter learned self-awareness competing in team sports. "Athletics taught me there are some things I do well, and there are some things I did not do well and it didn't take me long to learn that I was not the fastest guy in the world, and I would never be the fastest guy in the world, but I could still be a good football player. I'm just not going to be one of those guys with blazing speed now. You learn limitations and athletics teaches you in a hurry. You might not be able to dunk the ball, or you may be able to, but there are certain limitations you have to work around and get the job done."[103]

Another example of a trial and error experience was the lesson pastor Ken Fong shared from his role in high school student government, "When I was in high school I had two opportunities to be in student government. One was to be the senior class president and the other was to be the student body vice president. At that time I learned I was much happier as the vice president --and my take on that was, I work best when the buck doesn't stop with me... I'm an ideas person. I'm creative and I'm great at brainstorming and all that stuff. In order to be able to do that, I can't have the ultimate responsibility."[104]

#2. Getting Feedback on Paper (Assessments) (24 percent)

Feedback/affirmation involves learning from other significant people (like parents, friends, or teachers) about your areas of strength. Deepening one's understanding of self-awareness appeared to be influenced by the ability to learn from experience, not the other way around as mentioned in the meta-competency literature.

Assessments give us tools and categories for understanding ourselves and others. In our k-12 school systems, kids are identified as special needs, average (at grade level), or Gifted and Talented/High-Achieving based on written assessments/tests. When I was a kid they called the high-achieving group MGM --mentally gifted minor. I was in the MLTBIT group... Most Likely To Be In Trouble!

Fred Jantz, former senior pastor of Quail Lakes Baptist, shared how an assessment in high school had a very positive influence on him. "Sputnik had gone up in my freshman year, 9th grade, and there was a commitment to catch the Russians. So they started special programs and I think for the first time in my life somebody told me that I was a little above average so I got put into this special program. I think somebody identified me as having some potential. I did not view myself like that. I don't know if I really knew who I was. I was just trying to make it to the next thing, whatever the next thing was."[105]

#3. Getting Feedback from People (parents, teachers, bosses, coaches, and friends) (24 percent)

Steve Stroope shared about the way impact of getting feedback from parents made a positive difference with him. "My parents encouraged me to be myself. My two brothers and I are as different as night and day. My older brother is the token scholar of our family, you know he's got a PhD and speaks five or six languages and is just brilliant. My younger brother is just as creative as all get out.

My mom and dad have got a real good sense of who they are and they loved us so much that there was a kind of security and a self-esteem that was there, that allowed us to be ourselves and we didn't really have anything to prove."[106]

Fred Jantz's experience with a teacher's feedback was a big lesson. "My Latin teacher in the 9th grade said (I was still signing Freddy) 'you're getting to be a young man so we're going to make it Fred. We're going to get rid of the 'y" and she said something that I'll never forget it because no one talked to me like that, she said 'you're going to move on to another chapter of your life.' Initially it was a shock. It was almost like a mini rite-of-passage."[107]

#4. Critical Events like Failures & Setbacks (12 percent)

What influences change in self-awareness? "It

127

appears that critical events and role transitions may alter a person's identity or at least trigger personal explorations, which later leads to changes in self-awareness. In particular, failures and career setbacks have a powerful ability to make the person more self-reflective and more open to feedback from others. Failures and career setbacks have a powerful ability to make a person more self-reflective and more open to feedback from others."[113] Why did I get fired? Why did my kids rebel? Where did I go wrong? Why did my husband leave? "What doesn't kill you makes you stronger, right?"

#5. Convictions
Through many interviews following my initial study of megachurch pastors I found that breakthroughs in self-awareness are accomplished when our convictions outweigh and overtake our fears and insecurities. Conviction to have an impact, to be a better husband, a better dad/mom, staff member, and teacher were common. These convictions *must overpower* our fears and insecurities. Fears and insecurities are the arch enemies of self-awareness:

1. Defensiveness & Denial: "I've been wounded before on this and I don't want to be hurt again."

2. A Sense of Powerlessness: "I can't change" victim mentality

3. Low Self-Worth: "I don't like who I am, who I've turned out to be and it's too painful to even look too closely at who I really am."

Self-Awareness plus *Spiritual Wholeness*
Most of the current leadership development research would agree that self-awareness is one of those

qualities that is truly essential for impacting others. Self-Awareness is to be conscious of who you *are* and who you are *not*, to know what you are good at and what you are not. It is to see yourself as other people see you. However, in my original research I found that self-awareness was very important for leaders to know, but then after the research was completed I continued to interview high impact men and women about this. I eventually discovered there was something else in addition to Self-Awareness that was actually more crucial.

Some people can be very self-aware but can also be so massively insecure and highly defensive when issues come up that put the spotlight on what they are not good at, --where they have tanked in the past, or majorly blown it. I believe the key to truly seeing yourself clearly flows from a healthy spiritual life, a life of the soul, a kind of *Spiritual Wholeness.* This is so crucial to all of the other epoxy-like seams. It's like the lubricant in the machinery that forms self-awareness.

Spiritual Wholeness is an awareness of who you are and who you are not, an awareness of what you're good at and what you are not so good at, and being okay with it all! Completely OK! "Yep, you nailed it, that's me!" I love what Khalil, in the Veggie Tales Jonah Movie says about this: "My mother was a caterpillar and my father was a worm, but I'm OK with that."

With Spiritual Wholeness, you are fully aware of your strengths, weaknesses, failings, and overall weirdness, but you can be OK with that because your very identity is rooted in an emotionally rich, grace-filled, close relationship with Jesus. In this close relationship, you know that you are fully loved and embraced by the Lord himself, --just the way you are!

It's one thing to know your strengths, and to focus on them and what you are good at, but how do you respond when a new co-worker comes along who excels at your weak points? Or when someone throws your weaknesses up in your face during a performance review? *Are you OK with it then?* Spiritual wholeness helps us to be OK with it! Spiritual wholeness is so much more than a cerebral or purely theological understanding of the love of God for humanity. It is a cognitive *AND* an emotional comprehension, sort of like when you first found out someone has a crush on you.

Understanding spiritual wholeness is actually not very cognitive, but highly emotional. There may be some facts involved, like a love note, or a witness's testimony that the crush is a reality. "Dude, she really likes you!" When my wife Kirsten and I went our first date the experience was a major dud and disappointment. She was cordial but not really interested. The temperature in that restaurant dropped 40 degrees when she walked in! If they had cell phones back in those days she would have been on it all night. But then something happened about three months later. She gave me another chance and this time I knew something changed and she really liked me.

When I was a young architect, my boss and I were driving back from a job site and we stopped for lunch at the *Squeeze Inn* in Sacramento. He said his son knew the owner and their cheeseburgers were amazing. All I can recall is an enormous burger with a giant slab of cheddar cheese on it. It truly was amazing! I couldn't give scientific details on the quality of the beef or the temperature it was cooked to, or the cheese, or special sauce, but I know it was the best I have ever had! My response was much more emotional than cognitive. Spiritual wholeness is a lot like those cheeseburgers. When you taste it, you'll know it's amazing.

Spiritual wholeness is part of spiritual maturity, but it has its own distinctives. Spiritual maturity is the process where we grow in our relationship with Christ and develop the character of Christ in order to do the work of Christ. In the process of spiritual growth we become more patient, more kind, more compassionate, more courageous, and more bold, but spiritual wholeness is an age-appropriate sense of being close to God. At each successive stage of life we can experience a sense of peace, a sense of closeness to God, a sense that he is deeply in love with us, that we are one of His kids, His adopted daughter or son and fully belong in his family. We can live out of that identity in a way that honors Him and the family name.

Spiritual wholeness is more about understanding your spiritual family identity and living out of that identity. You are God's number one son, or number one daughter. He can say "I love you the best!" Just like he loves each of His children. Only God can say that because he practices a favoritism that makes each of us the focus of his love! When he thinks about you he breaks out in a huge smile.

Spiritual wholeness, as the word spiritual suggests, is about matters of the soul. It's common knowledge for those of us who go to church to believe that God loves us. Many of us can readily quote John 3:16 – "For God so loved the world...," or sing the song "Jesus loves me this I know..." but what is not nearly as common is to experience the emotional side of that love. To not just believe God loves you, but to feel it. I found my dad's old wallet not long ago digging around in the basement. My dad passed away over 25 years ago. You know what I found inside? Pictures of his grandkids. He loved and adored them. Jesus does not just love you; He likes you and wants to be with you. If Jesus carried a wallet He'd have your picture in it! That's how much He loves you! Authentic spiritual wholeness is in a sense a major internal reality check, and is about identity re-formation, seeing yourself as a deeply loved child of God.

We Have Become A New Person

Spiritual wholeness is a deep-seated, fully-saturated, growing awareness of the truth that as followers of Christ, we have become a new person. We have an entirely new identity with new perspective, new emotions, and new convictions about what really matters. Paul says in 2 Corinthians 5:17 "Therefore, if anyone is in Christ, he is a new creation; the old has gone, the new has come!" This is a statement of fact, not possibility, not a level to strive to, but a positional reality. This is true because anyone who has surrendered their life to Christ is a completely new person. You and I are *NOT* who we once were. The Bible says we used to be slaves, but now we've been bought with a price by Jesus Himself. We used to be dead in our sins and in rebellion against God and His ways. But now, we are deeply loved sons and daughters of God.

See what Paul writes about this in Ephesians 2:1-5, "As for you, you were dead in your transgressions and sins, 2 in which you used to live when you followed the ways of this world and of the ruler of the kingdom of the air... 4 But because of his great love for us, God, who is rich in mercy, 5made us alive with Christ even when we were dead in transgressions—it is by grace you have been saved."

How Do We Develop Spiritual Wholeness?

In Ephesians 4:22-24, Paul now encourages us to actively live out of this new identity, "You were taught, with regard to your former way of life, to put off your old self, which is being corrupted by its deceitful desires; to be made new in the attitude of your minds; and to put on the new self, created to be like God in true righteousness and holiness."

We are an entirely new person, "made alive" when we put our faith in Christ. Many of us know this truth cognitively, I am a new creation, I am a child of God, God loves me, etc... but often we live like Iron Man. Tony Stark steps into his Iron Man suit and he becomes "Iron Man" The Superhero. When he's not in the special suit he's old Tony Stark again. We need to put on the New Self and leave it on. WHY? "But because of his great love for us, God, who is rich in mercy, made us alive with Christ." It is the increasing flow of this knowledge, and our response of putting on the New Identity and keeping it on that fuels our Spiritual Wholeness.

We are not who we once were, --shown by the fact that God loves us so completely, so thoroughly, in spite of our past failures or rebellion. He longs for you and me to know how valuable we are to Him. Some of us come from families of origin where love and affection flowed freely and generously. This reinforces the truth of our incredible value to God. For others the setting wasn't so good. A parent's love may have been absent, or more conditional. If we did well in school, or scored points in the game, we would get love and affirmation. If not, we might get the cold shoulder, or maybe we would even get shamed.

Sometimes internalizing the love and affection of Christ for you may not come as easily. Knowing and experiencing God's powerful, transforming love is so critical to spiritual wholeness. We are not the first to struggle with this. The apostle Paul actually prays for this to happen in Ephesians 3:17 to 19, "And I pray that you, being rooted and established in love, may have power, together with all the Lord's holy people, to grasp how wide and long and high and deep is the love of Christ, and to know this love that surpasses knowledge—that you may be filled to the measure of all the fullness of God." Paul is telling us that God's love "surpasses knowledge" or is unknowable by human means. That's why he prays for God to help us grasp the weight of His love. When we know that someone important to us loves us, it changes everything.

Captain Kangaroo and Spiritual Wholeness

David Eckman, shared a moving story about identity in his book *Becoming Who God Intended:*

> Several years ago I read a summary of research on people who have survived and prospered even though they had come from heartbreaking backgrounds. The research said that the common factor with each person was that some adult had liked them and invested in their lives. That person might have been a coach, or a teacher, or relative. But it could have been almost anyone --though that "anyone" had to have been a person who looked upon them with love.
>
> The most remarkable story was told by very successful, mature woman who had come out of an abusive childhood. The person in her life was Capt. Kangaroo. In the hell that was her home, she would turn the TV on and watch the captain look back at her affectionately. She believed him when he smiled and said, "boys and girls you are special." She saw herself in his eyes, and she survived and prospered. Starvation for affection and the insatiable desire for a smile in the girl's heart made the words of the Captain life-changing."[108] "So much of sticking with things is believing you can do it. That belief comes from self-worth. And that comes from how others have made us feel about ourselves.[109]

How else does Spiritual Wholeness grow? It grows when we are becoming more like Christ (fully experiencing the new identity.) This *"Becoming"* is incremental *AND* a lifelong journey. The apostle Paul sums this "Becoming" up in 2 Cor. 3:18. Look at what he says to the Church in Corinth: "And we who with unveiled faces all reflect the Lord's glory, are being transformed into his likeness with ever-increasing glory, which comes from the Lord, who is the Spirit." God is doing a massive work of change and transformation in our lives. Paul is convincing the church in Corinth to live with their New Identity. "And We... are being *TRANSFORMED* into his likeness with ever-increasing glory." The Greek word in the New Testament for transformation is "Metamorphosis." You and I are being changed, morphed, and transformed from one state into another. This is a dynamic, fluid, process. The phrase "are being transformed" is not us transforming ourselves; it is literally another person acting upon us to bring about this change. It is much like a master potter is with clay, shaping, molding, refining a lump of clay into a beautiful work of art.

To Conclude

The "Becoming" of spiritual wholeness is not another Self-Help Program. It is a God-Help Program. Granted, we do have a role to play in this too. Paul is clarifying for us whose job it is to do what. In this case it's the Holy Spirit's job to cause and oversee our inner and outer transformation. In fact, the Lord Himself is far more committed to our becoming more like Christ than we are. We are being "transformed into his "Likeness," literally, 'his Image' which comes from the word "Icon' in Greek, a representative image. It's out of this new image, this new identity, that spiritual wholeness flows and is not forced. A life of high impact flows from spiritual wholeness

Remember, Spiritual Maturity is the process where we grow in our relationship with Christ and develop the character of Christ in order to do the work of Christ. Spiritual Wholeness is inclusive of spiritual maturity, but it's much more. Spiritual wholeness is a deep-seated, fully-saturated, awareness of the truth that we have become a new person. It's knowing who you are and who you aren't. Knowing what you're good at and what you're not and being OK with that. We are the apple of God's eye and He loves us with a love that never ends!

In the classic story *Beauty and the Beast*, the Beast used to be an arrogant, uncompassionate prince who dissed an old homeless woman who turned out to be an enchantress. She cast a spell on him and turned him into a beast. In order to break the spell he must learn to love another and then someone must love him in return. That someone must love him in return to break the spell... That's essentially what Jesus did for us. When we receive and experience his love for us it breaks the spell our old identity has on us and he then gives us a new identity. One that is rooted entirely in Him.

For Personal Reflection...

1. On a scale of 1 to 10, how would you rate your own identity awareness, emotional awareness, and impact awareness?

2. If you rated yourself and 8 or above, what do you think helped you rise to that level?

3. Do you consider yourself as having a strong sense of spiritual wholeness? If so, how did that develop? If not, what might be hindering that growth?

4. What could you do in the next year to help you develop more spiritual wholeness?

5. How might having spiritual wholeness influence your level of self-awareness?

Igniting Future
When you think about others you're investing in...

1. What percent of them have a strong sense of spiritual wholeness?

2. For those who are lacking in spiritual wholeness, is there anything you can identify that might be hindering their growth?

3. What are one of two concrete things you could you do more of to help them develop deeper levels of spiritual wholeness?

4. Are there any pre-spiritual wholeness things that may be necessary before solid spiritual wholeness can take hold? If so, what might they be?

Chapter 7

CULTIVATING AN AGGRESSIVE LEARNER MINDSET

You Really Are Your Own Best Teacher

When asked "who was your favorite teacher"? Most people can recall at least one or two. My high school US history teacher, Mr. Christiansen, was a captivating story-teller and helped me to foster a love for history. My college Spanish professor, I swear, had educational radar. Standing in front the class, she could look around the room engaging the students in dialogue, and she could tell if you were understanding the lesson, or if the lights were on and nobody was home. She was amazing! But no matter how inspirational, engaging, and pedagogically sound a teacher is, each one of us is still our own best teacher. We know ourselves like no one else and armed with the proper mindset and motivation we can teach ourselves almost anything.

After we moved from California to Wisconsin we realized that during spring break you better plan something out of state or indoors because you never know how cold it's going to be outside.

So one year we decided to go to one of those big indoor waterpark resorts in central Wisconsin. The place was amazing! They had so many different kinds of crazy waterslides and pools to swim in for kids of all ages, even us older ones. When I first walked through the doors into this expansive Wonderland of waterslides I noticed right away the *Flow Rider*. The *Flow Rider* was an indoor wave machine that duplicated you dropping down into a wave and riding it along the curl. There were mostly kids in line for this one with a few teenagers and fit looking young adults. But growing up in Southern California surfing, skateboarding, and bodyboarding I thought I would master that thing in a heartbeat. I could do this with one arm tied behind my back.

After doing a few of the other waterslides with my kids, I slowly made my way back to the *Flow Rider* and got in line. I watched each person in front of me wade out into the water, drop on their bodyboard, and slide down the wave. Some did it quite well, others crashed and burned.

When it came to my turn, I waded out confidently into the water, dropped on my board, slid down the wave, and was quickly washed to the side rolling over and over like a beached whale. It was a pretty embarrassing fail. Fortunately, my kids were not around to watch me embarrass myself.

However, I was undaunted, I got back in line, continued to watch others drop into the wave and I figured out what I needed to do to master this crazy wave machine. When my turn came, I stepped out into the water, with a little more humility than the last time, jumped onto my board and slid down into the wave, and kept riding the curl like I really knew what

I was doing! I learned from my experience, from my embarrassing failure, to come back into the water and do it right. Needless to say, my kids were not watching their old surf dog dad that time either, oh well.

Warren Bennis, leadership consultant to six US presidents, says the ability to learn as you go is the most important quality of a leader.[110]

Teaching and motivating people can be one of the most thrilling adventures, but it can also be most aggravating. Why do some people seem like born learners and others impervious to wisdom and knowledge? Those who make a difference in their world are aggressive learners. An aggressive learning mindset is learning as you go. This second epoxy-like seam ability is a meta-competency, because it increases your capacity to acquire other needed qualities or skills as you need them. Included at the peak of meta-competencies is the ability to learn from experience. It is a blend of personality, motivation, and learning tactics that influences an individual's ability to learn.[111] An aggressive learner mindset involves an internal drive and inquisitiveness, plus a down-to-earth common sense that keeps you, not free from mistakes, but less prone to repeating the same ones. This is an active and responsive, convictions-driven curiosity that fosters the humility and sensitivity needed to learn from life lessons as they arise.

Your capacity to learn from experience is also considered one of the most significant indicators of future high impact potential. Some people seem to naturally learn from experience, like sponges. Others have to work harder at it and eventually do learn things. But some never learn. "Men and women who remain effective over time are those who can learn from their experiences and use that learning to develop a wider range of skills and perspectives."[112]

Those who have a strong learning orientation tend

to rise much higher in organizational leadership positions. "A critical competency for successful individuals is the ability to learn, specifically how to deal with the changing demands of the environment and how to develop the appropriate new skills."[113] Similarly, McCauley and Van Velsor state "Executives who remain successful and effective over time are those who can learn from their experiences and use that learning to develop a wider range of skills and perspectives so that they can adapt as change occurs and be effective in a wider range of situations."[114] "Leaders are extraordinary learners... they are much better than most people at recognizing these lessons and using them."[115] Bennis, goes so far as to say that "the basis for leadership is learning and principally learning from experience."[116]

Shortly after we were engaged, I began to keep my own 'Kirsten notebook', where I would make mental notes about what she liked and disliked. In a sense, I was learning from experience about her preferences. One day, we were getting ready to go down to Balboa Island for a Balboa Bar, (one of the finest desserts Southern California has to offer). I was changing into a polo shirt, khaki shorts and top-siders. When I came out of the room Kirsten smiled, then frowned as she noticed I was also wearing argyle socks (just to see if she would say anything). In a kind, but firm tone, she just shook her head and said "Honey, No". When I busted out laughing she was genuinely relieved to see that I was not seriously style-challenged, but that I was doing it to note her response. My 'Kirsten notebook' was helping me to be an aggressive learner of my wife-to-be!

What Is An Aggressive Learner Mindset?
An aggressive learner mindset enables you to learn as you go. This epoxy-like seam is so influential that it is

like a gateway to increase your capacity to acquire other key abilities as you need them throughout life.

It also involves responsive learning from your environment, being ready for and alert to new opportunities to gain insights as you go. It can be a simple lesson like how to remove the old stain on my deck without disintegrating the wood, or how to change a tire when my Camry's custom wheel got a flat. The first time my car got a flat tire I was surprised to learn I needed an Allen wrench just to get the wheel covers off. So the next time I was at the hardware store I bought an extra one and kept it in the trunk just in case. It can be very practical lessons learned like when snowboarding, going from sunlit, soft snow to icy shade, you need to not edge as hard or you will hit the ground fast and hard.

These can also involve learning emotional lessons. When my dad died many years ago, I was working as an architect. One of my co-workers never said a word about it. He just ignored it, even though everyone knew I was off work for an entire week. Now, he was a younger guy and I'm sure didn't know what to say, so he said nothing. From that time on I learned to always try to acknowledge someone's loss, whether a loved one, or even a family pet.

Another lesson I've learned from experience is that my kids can hear much better than I think. In fact, they can hear the tone of my voice better than the actual words I say. They have a very finely tuned sense of tone and can discern whether I'm happy, sad, or mad, not necessarily by my words, but by my tone.

One common definition of insanity you've heard is "Doing the same thing over and over again and expecting different results." An aggressive learner mindset is the exact opposite of that. It is aggressively learning from your experiences day in and day out.

An Ancient Example

In the Old Testament book of Proverbs, ancient king Solomon writes a compelling example of the value of having an aggressive learner mindset. In Proverbs 24:30-34, he writes "I went past the field of the sluggard, past the vineyard of the man who lacks judgment." Solomon is describing walking down the road and he notices this vineyard that you can tell from observation is owned by a Mr. Lazy Guy. He describes the scene in more detail "thorns had come up everywhere, the ground was covered with weeds, and the stone wall was in ruins." The place was a wreck. Farm animals were most likely trampling the vineyard. But Solomon doesn't let this valuable lesson slip by. He says "I applied my heart to what I observed and learned a lesson from what I saw: A little sleep, a little slumber, a little folding of the hands to rest; and poverty will come on you like a bandit and scarcity like an armed man." What an aggressive learner mindset! He drew conclusions from what he observed of the trashed vineyard. He connected the dots to see that this place is not getting proper attention and therefore the owner must be a lazy bum.

An Aggressive Learner Mindset is about connecting the dots, making logical, causal connections in life circumstances and relationships. Notice what Solomon writes in Proverbs 27:12 "The prudent see danger and take refuge, but the simple keep going and suffer for it." This is learning as you go. Almost having built-in radar and the ability to make adjustments. An aggressive learner mindset involves recognizing new information, taking it in, and using it in meaningful ways.

In the spy thriller, *The Bourne Identity*, Jason Bourne is a CIA agent who has total amnesia. He has no idea who he is but is on a quest to find out. Even in his amnesia, he demonstrates an aggressive learner mindset. In the midst of this pursuit he hijacks a car and driver, then heads from Zurich to Paris. Midway to Paris they stop over at a roadside truck stop. Sitting at the table he begins to fill in some of the blanks in his identity. He says "I come in here and the first thing I'm doing is I'm catching the sightlines and looking for an exit. I can tell you the license number of all six cars outside. I can tell you our waitress is left-handed and the guy sitting up at the bar weighs 215 pounds and knows how to handle himself. I know the best place to look for a gun is the cab of the gray truck outside. And at this altitude I can run flat out for a half a mile before my hands start shaking. Now why would I know that? How can I know that and not know who I am?"[117]

He learned how to scan his environment so well it became unconscious and automatized. An aggressive learner mindset is training your senses to look for insights, for truth, for lessons needed to be learned. This is almost a holy curiosity, an inner desire to know *why?*

How Do You Cultivate This?

Where does an aggressive learner mindset come from? Are you born with it? How does it develop and grow? Why do some people have more of an aggressive learner mindset than others? Adults typically learn what they have to learn, or really want to learn, like a court-mandated anger management class or traffic school to avoid a spike in your car insurance.

One's motivation is critical. Most adults in the US are not avid readers. "In 2015, *43 percent* of adults read at least one work of literature in the previous year."[118] "A new survey on American *reading* habits reveals a statistic that's all too real: 27 *percent* of U.S. *adults* didn't read a single book within the last 12 months."[119] I found there are seven factors that increase the likelihood of becoming an aggressive learner.

Seven Factors to Cultivate An Aggressive Learner Mindset

1. A Strong <u>Conviction</u>:
"I Want To Make A Difference!"

Convictions are much stronger than beliefs. I've said they are beliefs on steroids. When you have the conviction to really make a difference with your life, a genuine internally fired drivenness to change your world, it will propel you to be an aggressive learner. To be effective in what you do requires that you keep learning how to be effective. Noted author and pastor, Leith Anderson, shared with me a story when he was first starting out as a senior pastor. He would not describe himself as a gifted evangelist, but he had the conviction that the Lord had called him and his church to reach people who were far from God. So he would go door-to-door sharing the Gospel with people who didn't attend a church, something that was way outside his comfort zone. He said, when it comes to evangelism, "you have to do what needs to be done." He learned that if he expected his church members to reach out to others he had to be an example.[120]

In my first official ministry job as a middle school director at Woodbridge Community Church in Southern California, my youth pastor, Bill Flanders, signed me up to go to a youth ministry leadership conference. I loved learning from these seminar leaders, who had a lot more experience than I did. Bill encouraged me to keep in contact with some of the leaders to continue to learn from them. A few weeks later I had lunch with Eric Heard, who was the middle school pastor at EV Free Church in Fullerton. I really learned a lot from Eric's workshop at the leadership conference. His middle school group was four times the size of mine. At lunch I learned even more about recruiting and developing your volunteer team. It was my conviction to reach more middle school students and to help grow their faith. That conviction massively fueled my need to aggressively learn how to accomplish that dual goal.

2. Spiritual Wholeness:
"It's not about me, it's about the mission!"

Spiritual wholeness is present when we know who we are and who we aren't, and what we're good at and what we are not and to be OK with that. When we are comfortable in our own skin this settledness gives us an increased ability to receive constructive criticism. When you have a good measure of spiritual wholeness you are much more open to advice and correction. Similarly, self-esteem plays a key role in a person's ability to learn. McCauley & Van Velsor noted "Individuals with high self-esteem seek more feedback because they feel they have less to fear from it."[121] They also said that "In order to learn, people must be strong and secure enough to make themselves vulnerable to the stresses and setbacks in the learning process"[122] Spiritual wholeness allows us to aggressively learn new insights in order to better accomplish our mission at hand, whatever that may be.

3. A Sense of Inadequacy:
"I don't know this, but I need to!"

When we can recognize a deficit, the awareness builds its own sense of urgency to do something about it. Pastor Joel Hunter credited a sense of inadequacy that was formative in his ability to learn from experience: "Well, I think the humble beginnings that I had was a big factor. I didn't have the best of educations, and had a long way to go, and still do, but

I think that gives you a sense of inadequacy, it gives you a teachable spirit. You don't have the philosophy that you know it all. And you can admit that you are inadequate there, and I need to learn there, and I think that that probably is a plus, that you have a teachable spirit."[123]

Similarly, Ken Fong credited a sense of inadequacy and insecurity to developing his ability to be an aggressive learner: "I had a strong sense of my own inadequacy, that I just don't have enough, and there is this growing awareness that I had to provide people with a more substantial theological foundation than what I had available. I was running into people for whom all those pat answers and all those easy apologetic answers weren't working, so when the easy answers weren't working I thought I needed something more substantial, more of the what, why, and how; that I could go down deeper and say this was it. I think with that sense of inadequacy and insecurity, I needed to be fortified because not only did I have an inordinate respect for intellectuals, but also an inordinate fear of being caught without having information."[124]

4. A Good Example:
You catch it from Mom or Dad, others you respect

Ninety percent of the knowledge we gain by watching others do something. One megachurch pastor in my study told me about how his dad would often go to the library get a book on something then read how to do it and then he could do it himself. He said he watched his dad build all kinds of things, fix all kinds of things, and learn how to do it just by reading a book." Those were the days before YouTube.

Kenton Beshore recalled how working for his dad helped to develop his ability to become an aggressive learner. "...We had a big piece of horse (property), so we built six corrals in the back of our yard. So, my dad would go, "OK, we've got to build six corrals." And we'd go get a post-hole digger. I'd dig posts. Then we'd get fence pipes from somewhere... and rent a truck, go pick up used pipes from some bizarre place. And then he'd go get a welder, and then he'd say, "Now, weld!" And I'd have to figure it out, because I didn't know anybody who could weld. And my dad figured welding would be pretty easy, so I'd learn how to weld."[125] There was a positive expectation that he would be able to figure out how to do things.

5. Little Wins: *Doing It Develops It!*
Learning is its own reward...

When we learn something new that adds significant value to our lives, it reinforces our openness to keep learning. I grew up in a family of golfers in Southern California. On the weekends, my mom and dad were always playing golf with my aunts and uncles. My dad bought me my first set of junior clubs when I was eight years old. Now golf is a lot more fun when you are improving. In order to improve you need to learn how to play better. As a teenager, I remember golfing with my dad, my Uncle Bill and my cousins one summer day. For the first three holes my Tee shot had a wicked slice to the right. I spent more time looking for my lost ball then playing golf. Around the fourth tee box, my uncle Bill suggested that I change my grip in order to compensate for the slice. I saw immediate improvements. Later that summer I asked my dad to sign me up for golf lessons so I could improve even more. The more we learn, the better it gets and the positive reinforcement of learning snowballs in a good way to reinforce an aggressive learner mindset.

149

6. God wants us to learn from advice!
The upside of listening to correction...

In Proverbs 12:15, King Solomon writes: "The way of a fool seems right to him, but a wise man listens to advice." Now discernment is needed to know whose advice is solid. According to one long-term study, the top two reasons for job derailment, getting fired or demoted are: one, failing to listen to advice and feedback, and two, refusing to change when change was needed (Acting on advice).[126]

Similarly, Solomon writes in Proverbs 15:31, "He who listens to a life-giving rebuke will be at home among the wise." Have you ever confronted a friend over a difficult issue only to have them totally blow you off? Where they are too defensive and just not listening to your seasoned advice? Sometimes, we take correction as such a big bummer, but the results can be life-changing. This was true for me years ago, on a church college group ski retreat (and I loved to ski. My license plate was "SKI UBET"). I was having a great time skiing with my buddies, trading off taking each other's photos doing back scratchers off of jumps, and not really engaging with the rest of the students on the retreat, just doing my own thing. Our youth pastor pulled me aside. I was technically supposed to be a leader in the college group. In a kind, but firm way, he basically told me I was being selfish and self-centered and needed to give attention to others in the group. By God's grace I didn't get defensive (my pride took a little beating though) and changed my attitude. In retrospect, I am so glad I listened to that correction, because that was one of those pivotal events that helped me become more other-centered over the long run.

Sometimes our critics can truly be the most helpful for our future success and impact. Has anyone ever told you that you talk too much, you're just a people pleaser, or that you don't follow through? How did you respond? Why is it that some people either *do not listen,* or *appear* to not listen? My top reasons people blow-off the advice of other's are:

1. Pride
2. Advice is given with an attitude so they discount the weight of it.
3. Advice does not seem relevant
4. The one giving advice does not appear credible
5. Preoccupation with something else, too much static from somewhere else...

Solomon says in Proverbs 25:12, "Like an earring of gold or an ornament of fine gold is a wise man's rebuke to a listening ear." To have a "listening ear" takes humility. When we are humble we are approachable. Humility is key to getting good advice. When we are humble, people will want to help you out. We all have blind spots and will always benefit from someone shooting straight with us. However, it's when we react defensively and arrogantly when given a rebuke, correction, or a critique, kind of a *"Who are you to tell me..."* attitude that ensures someone will help you once, but that's about it.

7. <u>Malleable Intelligence:</u>
It unleashes the motivation to learn!

Educators call this the Theory of Malleable Intelligence. I also covered this is in the chapter on primitive confidence talking about hard work. Malleable intelligence proposes the idea that superior students believe they can change, improve, and become more intelligent by working hard. As a result, they aren't limited by perceived natural talents or genetic factors. Nothing is more discouraging to a teacher than to see students with incredible potential quit trying because they believe they are just not smart enough.

This is not to say natural talents are not influential. They most definitely are, but when compared with a belief in the ability to improve through hard work, natural talents lose hands down. Multiple studies soundly reinforce this idea.[127] One need look no further than the world of sports to see recurring examples of hard work triumphing over talent – something that occurs often enough to show that it's not an anomaly.

To Conclude

An aggressive learner mindset can be cultivated. Some of the best communicators in the country demonstrate this by getting feedback on their lectures, talks, or sermons, in order to improve. Rene Schlaepfer, pastor of Twin Lakes Church in Northern California, learned the value of getting constructive criticism early in his career in radio:

> One thing I learned in radio, is that you have constant critique sessions, where the program director is always critiquing you and you learn to accept it objectively. One thing I see in a lot of church leaders especially is that they don't have any feedback mechanisms. They don't want them, or are afraid of them. I think in radio I really learned you are just dialed in to when your ratings come out. You can tell every quarter hour of every day what every demographic thought of what you were doing on the radio, whether the ratings went up or down, and you know, women aren't listening as much as they used to, or you got the teenage girls but no men, so you are constantly getting feedback. The program director says that you were telegraphing the punch line to that joke, or you weren't hitting the call letters hard enough. I think that, in retrospect, was a huge,

gigantic influence for what we do now because I'm not afraid to just go to look at the financial numbers, the conversion numbers, the attendance numbers, and it's not a matter of my needing my ego stroked, it is just a matter of what is going on. I think a lot of people are afraid of that or think that it is unspiritual.

Even when I go and preach at a conference or at another church, I always ask them, and say I need three people who work there to give me a critique after the first time I talk, and really blunt critiques, because otherwise, how can you get better? I still remember to this day, one whole talk that was critiqued and I completely reworked it because I thought some of the people just had great criticism, and you go 'why was I so blind and didn't see that myself,' but they are right.[128]

Personal Reflection...

**Aggressive Learner Mindset Assessment
(Check "a" or "b")**

1. When faced with a challenging situation:
____ a. I look for solutions, or
____ b. I tend to look for someone to blame

2. When it comes to receiving advice & feedback
from others:
____ a. I am open to it, or
____ b. I tend to be too defensive

3. My co-workers and friends would say:
____ a. I am a good listener, or
____ b. I talk too much

4. When I am in conversation with co-workers
and friends:
____ a. I enjoy the interaction, or
____ b. It is important to get my point across

1. Describe a recent occasion where you learned something on your own that you really benefitted from?

2. Can you think of a mentor, friend, or parent that modeled an aggressive learner mindset for you? What stood out to you the most?

3. From the chart above, are there any areas where you scored yourself a "b"? If so, what could you could do differently to help you shore up those areas?

154

4. What are two or three things you could you do more of to help foster this epoxy-like seam?

Igniting Future

When you think about others you're investing in...

1. How are you currently modeling an aggressive learner mindset for others? What could you do to more overtly do that?

2. Of those you're investing in, how would they fare on the adjacent chart?

3. Can you think of one or two things you could do to help them improve their scores?

4. Of the 'seven factors' in this chapter, which do you feel would be most helpful to encourage?

Chapter 8

BUILDING A PLATFORM OF BUOYANCY

Preparing To Stay Afloat Through Monsoon Season

Any parent of a toddler knows all about buoyancy. Shopping for the newest child-flotation devices, you are confronted with brightly colored shelves stocked full of floating swimsuits, triple-layered life jackets, and cartoon character swim tube trainers. However, being buoyant does not mean you never go under water. It means regardless of the storms and waves, you eventually rise to the surface.

Back in my early twenties I was working as a consultant for the Navy in San Diego to track the major overhaul construction of battleships and aircraft carriers. After weeks of climbing all over these ships I wondered "how do these giant hunks of heavy steel stay afloat?" "Why don't they just drop to the bottom?" One day at work as I was combing through the drawers of the old workstation I inherited, I found a textbook on Naval Architecture and Ship Design. In it I learned for the first time how the principle of buoyancy actually works. If you place a lead ball in a pail of water it will sink, but a plastic ball will float. Because if the weight of an object is greater than the weight of the water it displaces, it will sink like a lead ball, but if the weight of the object is less than the weight of displaced water, --like a ping pong ball, it will float.

Every vessel that has ever sailed on water, every submarine that has ever launched, all objects that come in contact with a body of water, are governed by the principle of buoyancy. This explains why Styrofoam-filled life jackets float on water, but chunks of concrete and steel sink. It also explains why it is possible to make ships out of steel. A stack of steel sheets will sink like a stone; but weld that stack of sheets into a shape that displaces more water than the weight of the steel (water is pretty heavy) and the object will float!

BUOYANCY

Now, being buoyant, in a leadership development sense does not mean you never go under water. It means regardless of the storms and waves, you eventually rise to the surface. Buoyancy is the ability to flex, adapt to, and endure major change, turbulence, and opposition. It utilizes wisdom and courage to both cause and endure change, without compromising your convictions. It is the discernment to resist being pulled into issues that are not essential or important. It also involves the capacity to persevere with a laser-like focus and tenacity to see things through.

Buoyancy is a critical epoxy-like seam, another gateway ability that opens the door to learn other useful skills and abilities as you need them down the road. When it comes to buoyancy, many things will float for a while, but in the long run they don't last and eventually sink. In 1967 in Nanaimo, British Columbia, they began the first annual bathtub race. They float for a while but not over the long run. Likewise, the world championship cardboard boat races are held in Heber Springs, Arkansas. These flimsy boats float for a while but not for long. We need the ability to stay afloat for the long haul.

At the heart of Buoyancy are two major qualities: Adaptability and Perseverance. To stay afloat you need to adapt. Adaptability is the wisdom and the courage to flex, change, or adjust without compromising core values. To stay afloat you also need to persevere. Perseverance involves a laser-like focus and stick-to-it-of-ness to see things through, to stay the course, to not give up.

What Is Adaptability?

Adaptability is the ability to change, as circumstances demand, but without compromising your core values. It is the wisdom and the courage to make the changes needed, and to modify your current approaches. It includes "flexibility, an openness to new ideas, dialogue skills, and being comfortable with change." It is "the ability to process new experiences, to understand them and integrate them into your life... In a sense, it is applied creativity..."[129]

Jim Collins & Jerry Porras in their classic leadership book, *Built to Last,* identified a key principle in highly successful companies: "Preserve the core, stimulate change." Guard the identity and purpose of the company, while at the same time encourage and welcome adjustments and updates. This was a quality of many prosperous companies that had stellar profits over the long-haul. In other words, stay flexible, but stubbornly keep your core values.[130]

The Apostle Paul

In I Corinthians 9, Paul displays an adaptability that preserves a core value and stimulates change. He says, "Though I am free and belong to no man, I make myself a slave to everyone, to win as many as possible. To the Jews I became like a Jew, to win the Jews. To those under the law I became like one under the law (though I myself am not under the law), so as to win those under the law. To those not having the law I became like one not having the law (though I am not free from God's law but am under Christ's law), so as to win those not having the law. To the weak I became weak, to win the weak. I have become all things to all men so that by all possible means I might save some."

Paul here is modeling both a winsome adaptability and a clear purpose. Paul's conviction and core value is to win others to Christ. *How?* By adapting his approach to his target audience. He realized if one way to communicate the Good News to Jews or Gentiles won't work in one place, he would try a different approach. He preserves the core value of winning others to the faith, but stimulates change by altering his methods.

Good Reasons for Becoming More Adaptable

When it comes to adaptability, or what Bennis and Thomas, call "adaptive capacity," they note, "to the extent any single quality determines success, that quality is adaptive capacity."[131] It is considered the signature skill of high impact people. Adaptability is considered crucially important to all branches of the military. "In the military, leaders are expected to seamlessly transition between training settings and combat settings."[132] Adapting from one setting to another is a matter of life and death. Similarly, "Improvise, Adapt, Overcome," is an unofficial slogan of the U.S. Marines that was made popular by Clint Eastwood's movie, *Heartbreak Ridge*.[133] "Academic content is not very useful in and of itself. It is knowing how to apply it in new situations or to new problems that matter most in the world of innovation."[134]

The Four Components of Adaptability
There are four components to adaptability. These four can often meld together so quickly as to be indistinguishable, and yet exist as separate entities. They are: Problem, Options, Discern, and Action.

1. **Problem Recognition:** Realizing we have a problem and need to change (something is not working)
2. **Options Invention:** Brainstorming options
3. **Non-negotiable Discernment:** Clarifying what should be immovable AND what should not (Which hills to die on? This is where we make career shortening decisions.)
4. **Action Oriented:** Having the courage to choose an option in order to adapt or stay the course.

David's Adaptability with Goliath
You can see these four components in the vivid account of the encounter between David & Goliath. In I Samuel 17, we see David's adaptability displayed as he takes out the giant, Goliath.

161

Goliaths Challenge:
"**10** Then the Philistine said, "This day I defy the ranks of Israel! Give me a man and let us fight each other." **11** On hearing the Philistine's words, Saul and all the Israelites were dismayed and terrified."

Little David Shows Up on the Scene and Recognizes the Problem.
"**20**Early in the morning David left the flock with a shepherd, loaded up and set out, as Jesse had directed. He reached the camp as the army was going out to its battle positions, shouting the war cry. **21**Israel and the Philistines were drawing up their lines facing each other. **22**David left his things with the keeper of supplies, ran to the battle lines and greeted his brothers. **23**As he was talking with them, Goliath, the Philistine champion from Gath, stepped out from his lines and shouted his usual defiance, and David heard it. **24**When the Israelites saw the man, they all ran from him in great fear."

David's Adaptability:
"Saul said to David, "Go, and the LORD be with you." **38**Then Saul dressed David in his own tunic. He put a coat of armor on him and a bronze helmet on his head. **39**David fastened on his sword over the tunic and tried walking around, because he was not used to them. "I cannot go in these," he said to Saul, "because I am not used to them." So he took them off. **40**Then he took his staff in his hand, chose five smooth stones from the stream, put them in the pouch of his shepherd's bag and, with his sling in his hand, approached the Philistine."

David's Success:
"**48**As the Philistine moved closer to attack him, David ran quickly toward the battle line to meet him. **49** Reaching into his bag and taking out a stone, he

slung it and struck the Philistine on the forehead. The stone sank into his forehead, and he fell face down on the ground."

In order to successfully survive this clash David had to adapt. First, David recognized Israel had a problem that needed to be addressed. For David, the problem wasn't Goliath as much as the fact that someone was daring to challenge the armies of the living God. When he accepted the task and was offered equipment, he immediately recognized a problem and needed to change. He recognized something's not working. The way we've always done it will not work. Second, he recognized he has options. He didn't have to do it the way they had always done it. He broke out of conventional wisdom. By flexing and adapting, David went with what he knew best. Third, he discerned what should be immovable and what should not move.

To follow the sequence, he first realizes that Goliath has to Go. There is no compromise here. Second, he believes that traditional armor is optional. He can flex and adapt on this one. Finally, he had the courage to adapt, take down Goliath, and stay the course. Where everyone else could only see an enemy too powerful to beat, David saw a target too big to miss!

Adapting in the Family

Parenting different personalities requires different approaches. It is possible to vary discipline approaches with kids without caving on our core values. For some kids, if we change our tone of voice that is enough. For others, we need to remove privileges for a while. Buoyant parenting demands we adapt.

Adapting On-The-Job

When it comes to leadership and collaboration in the workplace, treating people as individuals is key because there is no "one size fits all". We need to adapt and communicate differently depending on other's preferences and culture, again without compromising the core. In the early 1990's, when email was first coming of age, I learned a valuable lesson from a colleague who lived in the Silicon Valley. Whenever I would send her an email I typically started out "Hi so-in-so, I trust you are having a good week…" then after initial pleasantries I would get to my point. Then I would end it with a "thanks so much for your help, Tom." When she would reply to my email she skipped all the pleasantries and just sent the facts, no greeting, and no "have a nice week." She was all business. It came across to me as a little rude. Like she was mad, or in a bad mood. Now she didn't type in all caps or anything like that. What was also strange is that when we would meet in person she was very kind and thoughtful. What I learned was that she had a very different style of email communication. She cut right to the point. It didn't have anything to do with her mood or attitude. She had worked at other tech companies in Silicon Valley and developed her email style from them. It was my job to adapt, not shame her into compliance.

The Enemies of Adaptability

There are four enemies that hinder us from becoming more adaptable: low self-awareness, being too rigid, lacking discernment, and being too adaptable. These four can come and go throughout multiple life seasons:

First, having *low self-awareness* doesn't allow us to see the need to adapt and ask "Why should I change?" This is cluelessness at its finest. I found in my initial research interviews that most men didn't begin to experience significant levels of self-awareness until they were in their early forties. Prior to that time they intuitively focused on what they were good at and avoided what they weren't.

Second, *being too rigid* puts us in a posture where we flat out don't want to, and are not willing to adapt. "It's my way or the highway!" and we are not willing to pay the price, or take the risk to adapt. Sometimes, it's just too uncomfortable to adapt. Years ago, in the church where I was serving, we decided to change the service times in order to accommodate the growth in our adult Sunday school classes. If we changed the worship service times we could double the square footage of classroom space. At least one member was furious with this decision and started rattling cages. When I pressed him for the reason why he was so upset he said the new service times will make he and his wife thirty minutes late for brunch at their favorite restaurant and they will have wait in a longer line to get a good table. His rigidity and lack of self-awareness were stunning.

Third, is a *lack of discernment* which occurs when we make something a "divine conviction" that God may have never intended, either consciously or unconsciously. In other words, we die on the wrong hill. We choose the wrong battle. We listen to the wrong sources. When the Big Storm comes, knowing what to toss overboard and what to keep is critical. Before I made the transition into vocational ministry, I served as an elder in my church. One meeting a member asked to address the entire elder board over a concern he had. When he walked into the room that night he was visibly disturbed and began to lambaste the entire board over how he believed a beloved staff member was mistreated in a recent departure. Now this guy was an active member and relatively well thought of, but that night he became a loose cannon that rolled overboard. The big problem was that he failed to do a proper fact-check and was acting on fake news. After what seemed like quite a few minutes and he was done raking us over the coals, our elder board chairperson spoke up to clarify his misinformation with substantiated facts that were opposite of what he believed to be true. The guy was horrified and left the room in disgrace. Unfortunately he left the church as well. He displayed for all to see that night an astonishing lack of discernment.

Fourth is *being too adaptable*, where we are consciously or unconsciously a people pleaser. When you adapt and eventually do land on one option, one position, or one solution, you will *NOT* please everyone. For some of us that's hard to take. One of my former colleagues would get himself into trouble with this one all the time. He didn't know how to say no. One person would come to him with a controversial issue and he, wanting to please, would affirm that person's perspective. Then another person would come to him on the same issue but have an opposing take on it and he, wanting to please, would affirm that opposing take. When these people got together and shared notes they came to the conclusion that my colleague was a liar. Now, I don't believe he consciously set out to lie, but in his extreme people pleasing mode, when you did the math, he ended up sounding a lot like one.

How Do We Become More Adaptable?

In my initial interviews, I found the primary place people developed adaptability was in the midst of sink-or-swim situations. How many times are you going to face-plant in the same spot? In sink or swim conditions, necessity is the mother of invention. The challenges of life force you to adapt.

Clark Tanner noted how the challenges of farm life helped him to become more adaptable. "Growing up on the farm you had to be flexible. If it rained you had to change your plans. Animals die on you, you lose your pets, they get run over, and you have to adjust. I also think in working with people, that you have to realize that they are pretty fluid. They are going to change their minds; they are not going to necessarily think like you do. In work life, change is one of the things that is inevitable. It is going to happen, so you need to prepare yourself for it."[135]

Joel Hunter credited the challenge of losing his father at a young age and his mother's alcoholism as influential in his becoming adaptable. "With my father dying; my mother always off trying to earn a living and then later becoming an alcoholic, my circumstances were very unpredictable. You learn a couple of things. First of all, you learn how to read a situation *real fast*, because you don't want to be disappointed. After you're disappointed a number of times, then you develop the defense mechanism of, 'I'm going to stay ahead of the curve here.' So there was the, 'I'm going to read this situation, and I'm going to adapt to the best possible scenario. I'm going to go there before they get there.'"[136]

Ray Johnston's adaptability is motivated by his conviction to have a long-term impact in the ministries he launches. He does that by adapting. "I learned that it is easier to start something than to maintain it. I discovered that I can start something and get out of the gates fast, but at three years, we would not have the same vitality that we had at the start. I would say our youth ministry started with a bang, great stuff happened, we were two years into it, then it more leveled off, and had a little bit of a decline. I feel the same way about our next youth ministry in Marin.

Maintaining momentum is something I've thought a lot about. If you would have told me nine years ago that we will have the kind of momentum we have now, I wouldn't believe it. I've never seen anything like it, and it ebbs and flows a little bit, but I would say the last four months have been this massive rush. For me, that's a big growth area because, early on, I could start strong, but to do consistent growth over a long period of time, it takes years of wisdom. I don't know if I have it now, but I know I didn't then."[137]

When I interviewed Greg Laurie, senior pastor of harvest Christian Fellowship in Southern California, he shared that he grew up with seven dads in his life. His mother was an alcoholic, re-married a lot, and moved around too many times. In order to survive, he adapted and developed a good sense of humor and good relational skills that allowed him to connect with adults. "With seven fathers, and living in different environments all the time, being constantly put at brand new schools was normal. Just when I was getting comfortable and getting a set of friends I was uprooted and put in another school. I think in spending a lot of time around adults, not around kids for segments of my life I think I learned how to relate to different kinds of people, and to different ages of people at a very early age. My mom would have her friends over, and they would say "he's just like an adult that I can talk to," and I'd sort of entertain her friends. The thing was, is that I learned to adapt, and I learned how to be flexible." Similarly, Greg shared that "when you move around a lot and you're new all the time, you have to learn how to make friends quickly. I was able to go into a semi-hostile environment and sort of, with my sense of humor establish relationships with people. These are things I still utilize today."[138]

Now Adaptability is just one aspect of buoyancy. The second component is perseverance.

What Is Perseverance?

Growing up in Southern California and going to beach a lot I realized that the ocean can be pretty intimidating. You don't really know what's lurking below the water. When big waves roll in and toss you around they can make you feel powerless pretty quickly. If you panic, you are a good candidate for drowning. Whether you are surfing, bodyboarding, or bodysurfing, you need to know about the *washing machine effect*. When you get caught in the midst of a crashing wave, it will toss you around like wet clothes in a washing machine. You can get so disoriented you can't tell which way is up. Rather than flail around and panic using up all your air trying to break the surface of the water, the key is don't fight it. You just hold your breath, relax, ride it out, and eventually you rise to the surface. To survive, you have to persevere and wait it out. You have to stay the course and not give up.

We have an entire motivational industry today with books, speakers, and seminars helping people to achieve their goals. The number one reason people do not persevere and achieve their goals and dreams? It's not because they don't have decent goals and dreams, or their intentions were questionable, or their methods were inadequate. The number one reason is trading perseverance for the distractions, deviations, and detours on the side roads of secondary things. It could be the distraction of a bad news boyfriend, the deviation of a job that went nowhere, or the detour of getting the flu for a few days and then never get back on your workout regime.

The solution to distractions is perseverance. Perseverance helps give us a Teflon, non-stick coating against distractions & detours. It allows us to move through and beyond those challenges life throws us without them sticking to us and slowing us down.

To persevere is to have a laser-like focus and unflagging willingness to see things through. It is to lock on to your target goal until it's complete. It is about plodding, trudging, putting one foot in front of another. It is about running a marathon, not quick sprints. Some of the most high impact people are plodders, plodders with tenacity and focus. In Jim Collin's book "Good to Great," he and his team studied companies that excelled far above the norms, and they discovered the CEO's of those companies had very specific common qualities. These high impact leaders are called "Level 5 Leaders" and their two major abilities were a laser-like focus and tenacity to see things through to completion, plus a genuine personal humility that allowed them to get along with just about anyone.[139]

Four Great Benefits of Perseverance

There are many good reasons to develop perseverance. Even a semi-complete listing would fill an entire book. The first benefit is that *persevering helps you provide for the basic necessities of life.* Solomon writes in Proverbs 12:11, "He who works his land will have abundant food, but he who chases fantasies lacks judgment." In other words, keep your day job if you can, and work hard. A second benefit is that *when you persevere you are blessed by God.* This is a quality that the Lord himself rewards. In James 5:11 is says "As you know, we consider blessed those who have persevered. You have heard of Job's perseverance and have seen what the Lord finally brought about. The Lord is full of compassion and mercy." A third benefit is that *when you persevere you are obeying what God asks you to do.* In 1 Timothy 6:11 the apostle Paul tells us "But you, man of God, flee from all this, and *pursue* righteousness, godliness, faith, love, *endurance* and gentleness." To pursue here is to press forward or to aggressively run after. Endurance is a steadfast adherence to a specific course of action in spite of roadblocks. A fourth benefit is that *persevering helps us to make a difference.* Paul encourages us in I Corinthians 15:58, "Therefore, my beloved brethren, be steadfast (*lock onto*), immovable (*firm and unwavering*), always abounding in the work of the Lord, (*Why?*) knowing that your toil is not in vain in the Lord." You are not wasting your time serving God, but you are truly making a difference! Now one caveat: make sure you are locked onto what God wants, not simply what you want.

What Does Perseverance Look like?

Perseverance reveals itself in many forms. You notice it most when you've made it through a rough patch or accomplished a milestone goal. One recent study showed that only 80 percent of students graduate from high school in the US. That means 20 percent didn't persevere.[140] Only 33 percent of adults in the US have a bachelor degree or higher, and 67 percent do not.[141] Getting really good at a hobby or a sport doesn't happen without perseverance. On the job, if you are recognized by your peers as a go-to person for your expertise and competence it doesn't happen without you persevering in the same career field for many years. To put this in perspective, consider that it may take as many as 10,000 hours of honing a skill to move you from being a practitioner to a master. Many people hop from career to career, which at times is not all bad, but there are benefits to persevering and staying put. Staying married for the long haul is an excellent example of perseverance. Just ask anyone married twenty-five years or more and they will tell you about the ups and downs, the major happy times and the tough times, and the reward of persevering through it all. We have an amazing group of fifty-five plus age seniors in our church that meets for two hours every Friday morning for encouragement, worship, and teaching. Those people do not like to miss a meeting. I have visited many in the hospital, on the edge of life, early in the week, but if they get released in time, most will be there on Friday! They know how to persevere.

In his important book *How To Change The World: Social Entrepreneurs And The Power Of New Ideas*, David Bornstein describes social innovators as "people with new ideas to address major problems who are relentless in their pursuit of their visions, people who simply will not take 'no' for an answer, who will not give up until they have spread their ideas as far as they possibly can."[142]

During the Battle of the Bulge in World War II, the allied forces were getting pounded by a surprise German counterattack. The odds were drastically against them, but when the German army asked them to surrender, commanding general, Anthony McAuliffe, simply responded with one word "Nuts!" Allied forces persevered until relief came through.[143]

How Do You Develop Perseverance?

In my research I found many ways perseverance was developed, but three in particular rose to the top.

The third (11 percent) most mentioned way people learned to persevere was *the rewards and benefits gained along the way* reinforced the capacity to persevere. It was seen most in playing a sport, playing a musical instrument, and it is far more rewarding when you improve. This was also seen in going to college and completing a degree. This includes many rewards along way to graduation and the doors that open because of graduation itself.

The second (20 percent) most mentioned reason for developing perseverance was in the midst of *sink or swim situations*. This is where you've got to endure, hang in there, or you're going under. In James 1:3 it tells us that "...the testing of your faith *produces endurance.*" Similarly in Romans 5:3 it says that "...Not only so, but we also rejoice in our sufferings, because we know that *suffering produces perseverance....*" In one interview, Pastor Brad Franklin, senior pastor of Lakeside Church in Northern California, recalled that he needed the money as a kid so he went door-to-door asking for jobs. "Mowing lawns, I had to go knock on doors and say, 'Hey, would you like me to mow your lawn?' I had to keep going back, being persistent. I learned perseverance in that job as a kid."[144] In I Corinthians 9:24 Paul writes "Do you not know that in a race all the runners run, but only one gets the prize? Run in such a way as to get the prize." You've got to Persevere. A friend, who is in his forties recently shared a major regret. When he was a kid he quit the baseball team. He said he got mad at the coach, and felt he was unfair, only playing his favorites. So he just walked off and never came back. He never joined another team because he was so discouraged by that experience. He didn't persevere and regrets it to this day, three decades later. In many ways our convictions and values drive this. *How bad you want something* will often determine how long you will persevere.

The first (50 percent) most mentioned reason for developing perseverance was from the modeling of parents and other influential people. The modeling by the parents was clearly the primary influence reported for perseverance along with the influence of bosses, friends, team-mates, and coaches. In the book of Hebrews 12:1 it says "Therefore, since we are surrounded by such a great cloud of witnesses, let us throw off everything that hinders and the sin that so easily entangles, and let us run with *perseverance* the race marked out for us. The 'great cloud of witnesses' the author of Hebrews is talking about are role models from the Bible listed in the previous chapter (11). Those who have gone before us.

In our interview, Bob Russell noted that his parent's example was without question the major influence in his ability to persevere: "My dad worked at a factory. My mother worked at a Montgomery Ward's as a sewing machine sales person. My dad never missed a day of work. The example of perseverance that I would see in him, of following through, and then, if we did something at school, we weren't permitted to quit. You started something, you finished it. That was what Tom Brokaw called 'the greatest generation'. They had that sense of duty. That was really instilled in me."[145]

In another interview, Joel Hunter recalled the parental lessons that built perseverance: "I was never allowed to start a sports season and because I didn't like the coach, just drop out. I was never allowed to drop out of anything because 'We don't quit.' It's that simple in my family."[146]

To Conclude

To be buoyant does not mean you never go under. It means regardless of the storms and waves, you eventually rise to the surface. It is the ability to flex, adapt and endure major change, turbulence, and opposition. Buoyancy includes the wisdom and courage to both cause and endure change, without compromising core values. It involves the capacity to persevere with a laser-like focus and tenacity to see things through. See 2 Corinthians 4:7-9 for Paul's pictures of buoyancy.

Now, when it comes to adaptability and perseverance, some may be feeling a bit uneasy. "My parents were not good role models for me." Or "I've struggled with this my whole life." "I just seem to quit too soon." Let's see what the apostle Paul has to say to us about this in Colossians 1:9-11, "9For this

174

reason, since the day we heard about you, we have not stopped praying for you and asking God to fill you with the knowledge of his will through all spiritual wisdom and understanding. (*WHY?*) ¹⁰And we pray this in order that you may live a life worthy of the Lord and may please him in every way: bearing fruit in every good work, growing in the knowledge of God, ¹¹being strengthened with all power according to his glorious might *so that you may have great endurance* and patience..." Endurance and perseverance come from God, and it comes when we pray for it. Do not forget that God is more committed to us than we are to ourselves. He is the coach who never quits on us. I believe hope has a huge bearing on perseverance. Do you have the hope you can change? That with God's help you can persevere and make a difference? I believe you can. I believe God can use you to buoyantly persevere and impact others in ways you never imagined! Let me leave you with Paul's great words in Philippians 1:6, "Being confident of this, that he who began a good work in you will carry it on to completion until the day of Christ Jesus."

Personal Reflection...

1. In what ways has someone in your life demonstrated genuine buoyancy? Do you have any sense of what helped them to develop that over the years?

2. Do you consider yourself an adaptable person? If so, what demonstrates that capacity? If not, what might be influencing that?

3. Can you think of a 'hill someone died on', but they really shouldn't have? Just for argument's sake, what advice might you give them to help them become more adaptable and display more wisdom?

4. What is your own track record for persevering in the face of life's obstacles?

5. What is one "sink or swim" situation where you *had to* persevere? You had no choice! How did you feel when it was all over?

Igniting Future
When you think about others you're investing in...

1. Of those you're investing in, how buoyant are they? How is their track record for persevering or adapting? What evidence can you recall that supports your conclusion?

2. How have you modeled buoyancy to them?

3. What is one or two things you could you do to strengthen their ability to adapt?

4. If there are things hindering their ability to persevere, what could you do to help them overcome and strengthen their resolve to persevere?

Chapter 9

LEARN IT, ASSESS IT, SHORE IT UP, AND GIVE IT AWAY

How do people who are making a difference actually get that way? How do they ignite future and change the course of history one person at a time? They develop many layers of confidence, specifically, four distinct layers of confidence forged with the help of four specific epoxy-like seams (ELS). These layers and ELS's start to form in high school and continue to throughout life. The constantly morphing result is an even greater capability to live an outwardly focused life of influence.

Together, these layers of confidence and ELS's make a person stronger and bring about a lasting change and growth. The more layers of confidence and ELS's, the greater the capacity to impact others.

So how does this translate to reality? For new concepts to stick, it requires action. To *Ignite the Future* by helping to develop others into people of influence, demands action and engagement at the highest levels. Going full immersion with these four stages: Learn it, Assess it, Shore it up, and Give it away, are key to this kind of impact.

The first three of these stages involve taking your own deep dive into what you've learned, then self-assessing where you are with your own layers and ELS's, and next, shoring up any layers and ELS's needing attention. Then finally, giving it away to others, even as you continually refresh the first three personal stages. You don't have to be a '10' to give it away, but you do have to be honest with your own self-assessment and growth.

LEARN IT AND ASSESS IT

Chances are you already have a sense which layers and ELS's are more thoroughly developed in your life and which ones are not. Read through these brief summaries and assess your own growth. If you're having trouble assessing your own development then go back and briefly review the Personal Reflection questions at the end of each chapter to help you with this assessment.

Four Layers of Confidence

Primitive Confidence:
What They Really Need First

- Getting Really Good at Something.
- Four Reinforcing Factors (RF): Reliability, Priority-Driven, Hard Work, Team Work.

This layer of confidence most often forms first. This foundational component of confidence is directly related to getting good at something—attaining a high level of skill in one area. To become noticeably competent at something and gain a layer of primitive confidence you need four RF's working together to help you excel and sharpen your skills.

Assessing Primitive Confidence:
10 9 8 7 6 5 4 3 2 1
(Circle a number. '10' is high and '1' is low)

Four Reinforcing Factors of Primitive Confidence:

#1. Reliability, *Not* Inconsistency:
Making good on personal commitments.
#2. Priority-Driven, *Not* Impulse Driven:
Doing what needs to get done.
#3. Hard Work, *Not* Natural Talent:
Knowing that hard work pays off.
#4. Teamwork, *Not* Ball Hogging:
Seeing the value of people with unique strengths working together as one team. (See Chapter One for a full explanation of each RF)

Vicarious Confidence:
Discovering the Magnitude of Your Influence

- Model: Show me how it's done
- Affirm: Tell me I can do it
- Push: Challenge me to where I can grow

Vicarious confidence is something you get from someone else and give to someone else. It is a layer of confidence instilled from the outside, imparted from one person to another. (See Chapter Two for a full explanation of Vicarious Confidence)

Assessing Vicarious Confidence:
10 9 8 7 6 5 4 3 2 1

Command Confidence:
The Long-Lasting Benefit of Leading Almost Anything

- The Weight + The Win = Command Confidence

This layer of confidence comes when you are out in front and the weight of responsibility is pressing on your shoulders. It does not develop simply from leading something, but leading *well* and having a *"Win"*, receiving legitimate positive feedback on your performance. (See Chapter Three for a full explanation of Command Confidence)

Assessing Command Confidence:
10 9 8 7 6 5 4 3 2 1

Turbo Confidence:
The Reward Of Intense Life Lessons

- Fires Burn, You Cry Out, Help Comes, You Make it Through

Turbo confidence is forged during a short and intense period when life itself presses in to shape your character. It is formed through these trial-by-fire experiences as you call out to God for help, help comes from him, and you make it through. (See Chapter Four for a full explanation of Turbo Confidence)

Assessing Turbo Confidence:
10 9 8 7 6 5 4 3 2 1

Four Epoxy-Like Seams

Convictions:
Key Ingredients For Change

- Motivational Fuel & Moral Guardrails
- It is Absorbed (unconsciously) and Embraced (consciously) in Community
- 3-Part Center: Christ-Centered, Others-Focused, On-Mission

Convictions are very strong beliefs that directly affect your behavior. They are an epoxy-like seam that provides motivational fuel to accomplish great things. Convictions are also like compass points that guide you through moral landmines. Most often, you absorb and embrace them from others you admire. (See Chapter Five for a full explanation of convictions)

Assessing Convictions:
10 9 8 7 6 5 4 3 2 1

Self-Awareness and Spiritual Wholeness:
Correcting the Lenses of Self-Perception

- Knowing who you are and who you aren't and being totally OK with that because you know you are loved by God.

To have self-awareness is to see yourself as other people see you. To have spiritual wholeness is to be conscious of who you *are* and who you are *not*, to know intimately what you are good at and what you are not, and to be OK with that because of an emotionally rich knowledge that you are fully loved and embraced by God. (See Chapter Six for a full explanation of self-awareness and spiritual wholeness)

Assessing Spiritual Wholeness:
10 9 8 7 6 5 4 3 2 1

Cultivating An Aggressive Learner Mindset:
You Really Are Your Own Best Teacher

- You are your own best teacher.
- Humility and openness to learning from experience.
- Active and passive learning as you go.

An aggressive learner mindset involves an internal drive and inquisitiveness, plus a down-to-earth common sense that keeps you, not free from mistakes, but less prone to repeating the same ones. This is an active, focused, convictions-driven curiosity that fosters the humility and sensitivity needed to learn from life lessons as they arise. (See Chapter Seven for a full explanation of an aggressive learner mindset)

Assessing An Aggressive Learning Mindset:
10 9 8 7 6 5 4 3 2 1

Building A Platform of Buoyancy:
Preparing To Stay Afloat Through Monsoon Season

- Adaptability (Wisdom) + Perseverance

Buoyancy is the ability to flex, adapt, and endure major change, turbulence, and opposition. It also involves the capacity to persevere with a laser-like focus and tenacity to see things through. (See Chapter

Eight for a full explanation of buoyancy)

Assessing Buoyancy:
10 9 8 7 6 5 4 3 2 1

SHORE IT UP

Not all layers and ELS's are created equally. Some ELS's, like convictions and spiritual wholeness, help to open the door to growing the four layers of confidence.

Identify where you need shoring up, but then select one area to begin. Specifically define what's missing and brainstorm ideas of what you can begin to do to strengthen it. Who can you enlist to help you with this? The following questions will help you get started:

1. What's missing in your own growth?

2. What steps can you take to begin developing more of this?

3. Who can you enlist to help?

4. How will you know if you've made progress?

GIVE IT AWAY

Layers and ELS's grow at different rates and in a variety of environments. Some of the layers and ELS's you can directly give away, like vicarious confidence. But in most cases, intentionally offering them will increase the likelihood others will benefit from them when they are ready. The following suggestions give insights on how to best give that layer of confidence or ELS away:

- Primitive confidence and the four RF's: Help others find a place where they can excel at something, in a sport, performing art, or on the job. Guide them to hone in on a skill area they can improve. Coach them in connecting the 4 RF's to improving that skill.

- Vicarious confidence: You can raise the awareness of it to help others get it and give it away. What behaviors or habits can you intentionally model? Where are others you are coaching showing progress that you can affirm? Is there a training experience that will help them improve that you could suggest?

- Command confidence: You can raise awareness and provide incremental scaffolding experiences with the Weight + Win for others. What would be a good leadership role others could take on where their likelihood for success would be high?

- Turbo confidence: Teaching others about turbo confidence provides a readiness for adversity. "To be forewarned is to be forearmed." Adversity is one of the most formative forces in humanity. Our perspective determines whether it crushes us or transforms us.

- Convictions: Helping others develop these provides voltage for life. What convictions are you modeling that you want others to absorb and embrace? How could you intentionally teach these to others?

- <u>Spiritual wholeness:</u> When you help to cultivate this in others it opens the door wide for personal change and growth. It helps to remove emotional glass ceilings and roadblocks for upward growth. How could you teach spiritual wholeness to others? How could you coach them as they begin to develop this?

- <u>Aggressive learner mindset:</u> Fostering this in others allows forward momentum to build. Helping them to "Learn as you go" will be a life-long benefit. Are you modeling this as you share your own new lessons? How could you coach others in a specific area to benefit from learning as they go?

- <u>Buoyancy:</u> Encouraging this provides a kind of long term spiritual health insurance and influence and impact over the long haul. Is there an area someone you are coaching is 'stuck' or facing a significant obstacle? Use that area to walk them through options of ways they could adapt and overcome. Share your own stories of how you adapted and preserved to overcome a major obstacle.

So, Learn it, Assess it, Shore it up, and Give it away!

Who can you begin to give this away to? What will you do to start? How will you know if you're making progress? How can you change the course of history one person at a time?

Our first grandchild has just recently arrived and though she's only three months old, I can't wait to take her to Disneyland. I still love the inspiration the

Magic Kingdom brings to all ages. I know Tomorrowland will be different than the one I grew up with, but that's OK because I have a dream to *ignite future*, to sway what happens tomorrow by investing in the next generation who can ignite that future!

BIBLIOGRAPHY

Bandura, A. (1997). *Self-Efficacy: The exercise of control.* New York: W. H. Freeman & Company.

Bennis, W. G. (1989, 2003). *On becoming a leader.* Cambridge, MA: Perseus Books.

Bennis, W. G., & Thomas, R. J. (2002). *Geeks and geezers: How era, values, and defining moments shape leaders.* Boston: Harvard Business School Press.

Briscoe, J. P., & Hall, D. T. (1999). Grooming and picking leaders using competency frameworks: do they work? An alternative approach and new guideline for practice. *Organizational Dynamics, Autumn 1999,* 37-51.

Brooks, D. (2011) *The Social Animal, The Hidden Sources of Love, Character, and Achievement.* New York: Random House.

Burnett, B. & Evans, D. (2016). *Designing your Life: How to build a well lived, joyful life.* New York: Alfred A. Knopf

Clinton, J. R. (1988). *The making of a leader: recognizing the lessons and stages of leadership development.* Colorado Springs, CO: Navpress Publishers.

Collins, J., & Porras, J. (1994). *Built To Last: Successful Habits of Visionary Companies.* New York: HarperBusiness; 3rd ed.

Collins, J. (2001). *Good to great.* New York: Harper Collins Publishing.

Day, D. V., & O'Connor, P. M. (2003). Leadership development: Understanding the process. In S. E. Murphy, & Riggio, R. E.

(Ed.), *The future of leadership development* (pp. 279-311). Mahwah, NJ: Lawrence Erlbaum Associates.

Duckworth, A. & Seligman, M. (2005) *Self-Discipline Outdoes IQ in Predicting Academic Performance of Adolescents*, Journal of Psychological Science, Vol. 16, number 12.

Duckworth, A. (2016). *Grit: The power of passion and perseverance*. New York: Scribner.

Dweck, C. (2000) *Self-Theories: Their Role In Motivation, Personality, And Development*. New York: Psychology Press.

Eckman, D. (2005). *Becoming Who God Intended*. Portland: Harvest House Publishers.

Fiorina, C. (2006) *Tough Choices, A Memoir*. New York: Penguin Group.

Friberg, B., Mille, N., & Friberg, T. (2005) *Analytical Lexicon of the Greek New Testament* Bloomington: Trafford House Publishing.

Glaser, M. T. H., Chi, R., Farr, M. J., & Glaser, R. (1988). *The nature of expertise*. Hillsdale, NJ.: Lawrence Erlbaum Associates, Publishers.

Goleman, D. (2012) Emotional Intelligence: *Why It Can Matter More Than IQ*. New York: Random House.

Goleman, D., Boyatzis, R., & Mckee, A. (2002). *Primal leadership: learning to lead with emotional intelligence*. Boston: Harvard Business School Press.

Hall, D. T. (2004). Self-confidence and leader performance. *Organizational Dynamics, 33*(3), 254-274.

Hartford Seminary. (2004). *Database of megachurches in the US*. Retrieved March 2005, http://hirr.hartsem.edu/org/faith_megachurches_database.html

Klein, K. J., & Ziegert, J. C. (2004). Leader development and change over time: A conceptual integration and exploration of research challenges. In D. V. Day, Zaccarro, S. J., & Halpin, S. M. (Ed.), *Leader development for transforming organizations* (pp.359-381). Mahwah, NJ: Lawerence Erlbaum Associates, Publishers.

McCall, M. W. & Hollenbeck, G. (2002) *Developing Global Executives*. Brighton: Harvard Business School Press.

McCall, M. W. (1998). *High flyers: developing the next generation of leaders*. Boston, MA: Harvard Business School Press.

McCall, M. W., Lombardo, M. M., & Morrison, A. M. (1988). *The lessons of experience*. New York: The Free Press.

McCauley, C. D., & Van Velsor, E. (Ed.). (2004). *The Center for Creative Leadership handbook of leadership development*. San Francisco: Jossey-Bass, Inc.

Meredith, M. (1997) *Nelson Mandela, A Biography*. New York: St. Martins Press.

Northouse, P. G. (2004). *Leadership theory and practice* (Third ed.). Thousand Oaks, CA: Sage Publications.

Personal histories. (2001). Personal histories. *Harvard Business Review*, 27-38.

Powell, C. & Persico, J. (1995) *My American Journey: Colin Powell*. New York: Random House.

Price, S. (2018). *The Best Advice Ever Given, life lessons for success in the real world.* New York: Lyon Press.

Sorcher, M., & Brant, J. (2002). Are you picking the right leaders? *Harvard Business Review*, 78-85.

Thatcher, M. (1995). *Margaret Thatcher, The Path To Power.* New York: Harper Collins Publishers.

Tunnicliff, T. H. (2016). *How pastors grow into leaders: The early formative experiences of highly effective senior pastors.* Createspace.org publishers.

Wilson, T. D. (2012) *Revising Your Story*, http://www.apa.org/monitor/2012/03/revising.aspx, accessed May 28, 2018.

Wong, L., Bliese, P., & McGurk, D. (2003). Military leadership a context specific review. *Leadership Quarterly, 14*, 657-692.

Zaccaro, S. J., Day, D., & Halpin, S. (2004) *Leader Development for Transforming Organizations.* New York: Psychology Press.

END NOTES

Introduction

[1]Melvin Sorcher and James Brant, Are you picking the right leaders? *Harvard Business Review*, (2002): 79.

[2] Tom Tunnicliff, *The Early Leadership Development Experiences Of Highly Effective Senior Pastors* (A Dissertation at the University of Southern California, 2005)

[3] Hartford Seminary *Database of megachurches in the US*. Accessed March 2005, http://hirr.hartsem.edu/org/faith_megachurches_database.html (2004)

[4] J. C. La Rue, *Profile of Today's Pastor*. Accessed July 10, 2004, http://www.christianitytoday.com/leaders/newsletter/cln01025.html (2000)

[5] My single criterion was that each leader had to have grown a church close to 2,000 attendees, as opposed to those who took over as senior pastors of existing large churches or megachurches. While there are a number of qualities you can use to measure senior pastor effectiveness, for these first forty interviews, size was essential. The basis for my decision centered on the assumption that those senior pastors who had grown a church to at least 2,000 attendees had a track record of demonstrated leadership success and have in fact developed specific leadership capacities.

[6]American Plywood Association Website, Accessed Feb 10, 2011) http://www.apawood.org/level_b.cfm?content=prd_glu_main

[7] Stuart Briscoe, Senior Pastor Emeritus *Elmbrook Church in Brookfield, Wisconsin*, in an interview with the author, 2005.

[8] Ibid.,

[9] Leonard Wong, Paul Bliese, and Dennis McGurk, Military Leadership a Context Specific Review. *Leadership Quarterly, 14*, (2003) 657-692.

[10] Peter G. Northouse, *Leadership Theory and Practice*. (Thousand Oaks: Sage Publications, 2004)

Chapter 1

[11] Albert Bandura, *Self-Efficacy: The Exercise of Control* (New York: W. H. Freeman & Company, 1997), 34.

[12] Tom Tunnicliff, *The Early Leadership Development Experiences Of Highly Effective Senior Pastors.*

[13] Clark Tanner, Former Senior Pastor of *Beaverton Christian Church in Beaverton, Oregon,* in an interview with the author, 2005.

[14] Joel Hunter, Former Senior Pastor of *Northland Church in Lake County, Florida,* in an interview with the author, 2005.

[15] Angela Duckworth, *Grit: The Power Of Passion And Perseverance* (New York: Scribner, 2016), 235.

[16] Tom Tunnicliff, *The Early Leadership Development Experiences Of Highly Effective Senior Pastors.*

[17] Margaret Thatcher, *Margaret Thatcher, The Path To Power,* (New York: Harper Collins Publishers, New York, 1995), 9.

[18] Ken Fong, Senior Pastor of *Evergreen Baptist Church in Los Angeles,* in an interview with the author, 2005.

[19] Michael Foss, Former Senior Pastor of *Prince of Peace Lutheran in Burnsville, Minnesota,* in an interview with the author, 2005.

[20] Ibid.,

[21] Angela Duckworth, 225.

[22] Michelene Chi, Marshall Farr, and Robert Glaser, *The Nature of Expertise* (Hillsdale: Lawrence Erlbaum Associates, Publishers, 1988)

[23] Clark Tanner, Interview

[24] Bob Russell, Former Senior Pastor of *Southeast Christian Church in Louisville, Kentucky,* in an interview with the author, 2005.

[25] Angela Duckworth and Martin Seligman, *Self-Discipline Outdoes IQ in Predicting Academic Performance of Adolescents,* Journal of Psychological Science, Vol. 16, number 12, (2005) 44

[26] Tom Tunnicliff, *The Early Leadership Development Experiences Of Highly Effective Senior Pastors.*

[27] Carol Dweck, *Self-Theories: Their Role In Motivation, Personality, And Development.* (New York: Psychology Press, 2000)

[28] Ibid.,

[29] Angela Duckworth, 45.

[30] Angela Duckworth, 46.

[31] Colin Powell and Joseph Persico, (1995) *My American Journey: Colin Powell,* (New York: Random House, 1995), 29.

[32] Angela Duckworth, 42.

[33] Angela Duckworth, 120.

[34] Angela Duckworth, 137.

Chapter 2

[35] Martin Meredith, *Nelson Mandela, A Biography*, (New York: St. Martins Press, 1997), 10.

[36] Angela Duckworth, 84.

[37] Morgan McCall, Michael Lombardo, and Ann Morrison, *The Lessons of Experience* (New York: The Free Press, 1988), 72.

[38] I Timothy 4:12, NLT

[39] Barbara Friberg, Neva Mille, and Timothy Friberg, *Analytical Lexicon of the Greek New Testament* (Bloomington: Trafford House Publishing, 2005)

[40] Ray Johnston, Senior Pastor *Bayside Church in Granite Bay, California,* in an interview with the author, 2005.

[41] Kenneth Ulmer, Bishop, *Faithful Central Bible Church, in Los Angeles*, in an interview with the author, 2005.

[42] Ulmer, Interview

[43] Ibid.,

[44] Carly Fiorina, *Tough Choices, A Memoir,* (New York: Penguin Group, 2006), 21.

[45] Raul Reis, Senior Pastor *Calvary Chapel, Golden Springs, in Diamond Bar, California,* in an interview with the author, 2005.

[46] McCall, Lombardo, and Morrison, *The Lessons of Experience,* 69.

[47] Ibid.,

[48] Ibid.,

Chapter 3

[49] *Band of Brothers*, HBO TV mini-series, 2001

[50] Albert Bandura, *Self-Efficacy: The Exercise of Control,*

[51] Ken Fong, Interview

[52] Kenton Beshore, Senior Pastor *Mariners Church of Irvine, California,* in an interview with the author, 2005.

[53] Kenneth Ulmer, Interview

[54] Steve Stroope, Lead Pastor Lakepointe Church in Rockwall, Texas, in an interview with the author, 2005.

[55] Bill Coyne, Former President and CEO of Raley's Grocery Stores, in an interview with the author, 2011.

[56] McCall, Lombardo, and Morrison, *The Lessons of Experience,*

[57] Katherine Klein and Jonathan Ziegert, Leader development and change over time: A conceptual integration and exploration of research challenges. In D. V. Day, Zaccarro, S. J., & Halpin, S. M. (Ed.), *Leader*

Development for Transforming Organizations. (Mahwah: Lawerence Erlbaum Associates, Publishers, 2004), 9.

[58] McCall, Lombardo, and Morrison, *The Lessons of Experience,*
[59] Ibid.,
[60] Ibid.,
[61] Klein and Ziegert, Leader Development and Change Over Time, 365.
[62] McCall, Lombardo, and Morrison, *The Lessons of Experience,* 65.
[63] Hoosiers, Directed by David Anspaugh. Los Angeles: Hemdale Film Corporation, 1986.

Chapter 4

[64] Angela Duckworth, 252.
[65] Michael Foss, Interview
[66] Tom Tunnicliff, *The Early Leadership Development Experiences Of Highly Effective Senior Pastors.*
[67] Larry Adams, Senior Pastor of *Golden Hills Community Church in Northern California*, in an interview with the author, 2005.
[68] McCall, Lombardo, and Morrison, *The Lessons of Experience,*
[69] Ibid.,
[70] Ibid.,
[71] Morgan McCall and George Hollenbeck, *Developing Global Executives* (Brighton: Harvard Business School Press, 2002)
[72] Tom Tunnicliff, *The Early Leadership Development Experiences Of Highly Effective Senior Pastors*
[73] Hebrews 13:5 (NIV)

Chapter 5

[74] "According to a National Foundation for Credit Counseling online poll, if confronted with an unexpected bill of $1,000, only 36% of respondents would be able to tap an emergency fund." http://www.nfcc.org/NewsRoom/newsreleases/FLOI_July2011Results_FINAL.cfm, Accessed September 2011
[75] Jack Graham, Senior Pastor of *Prestonwood Baptist Church in Dallas, Texas*, in an interview with the author, 2005.
[76] Isaiah 50:7 NLT
[77] Bill Burnett and Dave Evans, *Designing Your Life: How To Build A Well Lived, Joyful Life,* (New York: Alfred A. Knopf, 2016), 43.
[78] *Moral Education,* http://gger.uic.edu/~inucci/MoralEd/overviewtest.html Accessed 2012

[79] David Brooks, *The Social Animal, The Hidden Sources of Love, Character, and Achievement* (New York: Random House, 2011) 128.
[80] Personal histories. (2001). Personal histories. *Harvard Business Review*, 27-38.
[81] Ibid.,
[82] Angela Duckworth, 163.
[83] Bob Russell, Interview
[84] Harley Allen, Former Senior Pastor *Calvary Temple Church in Concord, California*, in an interview with the author, 2005.
[85] Joel Hunter, Interview
[86] Larry Osborne, Lead Pastor *North Coast Church, Vista, California*, in an interview with the author, 2005.
[87] Timothy D. Wilson, *Revising Your Story*, http://www.apa.org/monitor/2012/03/revising.aspx, accessed May 28, 2018.
[88] Aristotle, *Nicomachean Ethics* Martin Ostwald, trans. (New York: Macmillan, 1962), 34-35.
[89] Mark Twain, *Two of the Most Important Days*, http://marktwainstudies.com/the-apocryphal-twain-the-two-most-important-days-of-your-life/ Accessed May 28, 2018

Chapter 6

[90] Socrates, Know Thyself, https://www.philosophybasics.com/philosophers_thales.html Accessed May 28, 2018
[91] Juvenal, Know Thyself https://en.wikipedia.org/wiki/Know_thyself Accessed May 28, 2018
[98] Proverbs 14:8 NLT
[93] Steven Price, *The Best Advice Ever Given, Life Lessons for Success in the Real World*, (New York: Lyon Press, 2018)
[100] Daniel Goleman, Richard Boyatzis, Annie Mckee, *Primal Leadership: Learning to Lead with Emotional Intelligence* (Boston: Harvard Business School Press, 2002)
[101] Goleman, Boyatzis, and McKee, *Primal Leadership*
[96] Douglas Hall, Self-Confidence and Leader Performance. *Organizational Dynamics, 33*(3), 254-274.
[97] Ibid.,
[98] Daniel Goleman, Emotional Intelligence: *Why It Can Matter More Than IQ* (New York: Random House, 2012)
[99] Ibid.,
[100] Ibid.,

[101] Clark Tanner, Interview.

[102] Ibid.,

[103] Joel Hunter, Interview

[104] Ken Fong, Interview

[105] Fred Jantz, Former Senior Pastor of *Quail Lakes Baptist Church in Stockton, California,* in an interview with the author, 2005.

[106] Steve Stroope, Interview

[107] Fred Jantz, Interview

[108] David Eckman, Becoming Who God Intended (Portland: Harvest House Publishers, 2005)

[109] Angela Duckworth, 209.

Chapter 7

[110] Warren Bennis, *On Becoming a Leader* (Cambridge: Perseus Books, 2003)

[111] Cynthia McCauley, and Ellen Van Velsor, Eds., *The Center for Creative Leadership Handbook of Leadership Development.* (San Francisco: Jossey-Bass, 2004)

[112] McCauley and Van Velsor, *The Center for Creative Leadership Handbook of Leadership Development*, 208.

[113] Stephen Zaccaro, David Day, Stanley Halpin, Leader Development for Transforming Organizations (New York: Psychology Press, 2004), 18.

[114] McCauley and Van Velsor, *The Center for Creative Leadership Handbook of Leadership Development*, 208.

[115] Noel Tichy, *The leadership engine: How companies build leaders at every level* (New York: Harper Collins, 1997), 59.

[116] Warren Bennis, *On Becoming A Leader,* 176.

[117] The Bourne Identity, Directed by Doug Liman. Santa Monica: Kennedy/Marshall, 2002.

[118] *The Long Steady Decline of Reading,* https://www.washingtonpost.com/news/.../the-long-steady-decline-of-literary-reading/ Accessed May 28, 2018

[119] *American Adults Don't Read* https://www.smithsonianmag.com/.../27-percent-american-adults-didnt-read-single-book-last-year- 180957029/ Accessed May 28, 2018

[120] Leith Anderson, Former Senior Pastor of *Wooddale Church in Eden Prairie, Minnesota,* in an interview with the author, 2005.

[121] McCauley and Van Velsor, *The Center for Creative Leadership Handbook of Leadership Development*, 209.

[122] *Ibid.,*

[123] Joel Hunter, Interview
[124] Ken Fong, Interview
[125] Kenton Beshore, Interview
[126] McCall, *Lessons of Experience*
[127] Carol Dweck, *Self-Theories: Their Role In Motivation, Personality, And Development.* (New York: Psychology Press, 2000)
[128] Rene Schlaepfer, Pastor *Twin Lakes Church in Aptos, California*, in an interview with the author, 2005.

Chapter 8

[129] Jon Briscoe and Douglas Hall, Grooming and picking leaders using competency frameworks: do they work? An alternative approach and new guideline for practice. *Organizational Dynamics, Autumn 1999*, 49.
[130] Jim Collins and Jerry Porras, *Built To Last: Successful Habits of Visionary Companies*, (New York: HarperBusiness; 3rd ed, 1994), 80-90.
[131] Warren Bennis and Robert Thomas, Bennis, *Geeks and Geezers: How Era, Values, and Defining Moments Shape Leaders* (Boston: Harvard Business School Press, 2002), 91.
[132] Leonard Wong, Paul Bliese, and Dennis McGurk, Military Leadership: A Context Specific Review. *Leadership Quarterly, (2003) 14*, 683.
[133] Heartbreak Ridge, Directed by Clint Eastwood. Burbank: Malpaso Productions, 1986.
[134] Tony Wagner, *Creating Innovators: The Making Of Young People Who Will Change The World,* (New York: Scribner, 2012), 52.
[135] Clark Tanner, Interview
[136] Joel Hunter, Interview
[137] Ray Johnston, Interview
[138] Greg Laurie, Senior Pastor of *Harvest Christian Fellowship in Riverside, California*, in an interview with the author, 2005.
[139] Jim Collins, *Good to Great: Why Some Companies Make the Leap and Others Don't,* (New York: HarperCollins Publishers, 2001), 17-35.
[140] *Why Students Drop Out,* https://www.huffingtonpost.com/2014/05/21/why-students-dropout_n_5365949.html Accessed March 15, 2018.
[141] *More Americans Have College Degrees Than Ever Before,* http://thehill.com/homenews/state-watch/326995-census-more-

americans-have-college-degrees-than-ever-before Accessed March 30, 2018.

[142] Tony Wagner, 101.

[143] McAuliffe, Jr., Kenneth, "The story of NUTS! Reply" The story of NUTS! Article The United States Army, United States Army. Retrieved June 28, 2017.

[144] Brad Franklin, Senior Pastor of *Lakeside Church, Folsom, California*, in an interview with the author, 2005.

[145] Bob Russell, Interview

[146] Joel Hunter, Interview